Excel

ADVANCED SKILLS

MATHS

YEAR 2

AGES 7–8

ADVANCED MATHEMATICS

PASCAL PRESS

Tanya Dalgleish

Written for the NSW Curriculum and the Australian Curriculum Version 9.0

Reprinted 2025

ISBN 978 1 74125 655 0

Pascal Press
PO Box 250
Glebe NSW 2037
www.pascalpress.com.au

Publisher: Vivienne Joannou
Project editor: Rosemary Peers
Edited and proofread by Rosemary Peers
Answers checked by Melinda Amaral
Cover and page design by Sonia Woo
Typeset by Julianne Billington
Printed by Vivar Printing/Green Giant Press

The publisher thanks the Royal Australian Mint for granting permission to use Australian currency coin designs in this book.

Contents

Introduction

The aim of the ***Excel*** Advanced Skills: Advanced Mathematics series is to build on and extend students' skills in Mathematics. Each book in the series supports the requirements of the Australian Curriculum (Mathematics) at each year level.

The series consists of six books, one for each year level, from Year 1 to Year 6. The series is supported by other books in the ***Excel*** Mathematics range.

- There are 30 units of work.
- Units that are even numbered have two parts: Units A and B.
- Units that are odd numbered have four parts: Units A, B, C and D.
- Students should work through the 30 units in sequence because the knowledge and skills introduced in one unit are consolidated and built on in subsequent units.

Units A and B: Focus on practice

- These units cover all the strands of the Mathematics Curriculum: Number, Algebra, Measurement, Space, Statistics and Probability.
- Each unit contains 14 questions.
- The question numbers cover the same topics in each unit (e.g. Unit A question 12 is always a subtraction question; Unit B question 4 is always a money question). The questions become progressively more difficult as students work through the book. This scope and sequence provides for regular practice that will extend the mathematics skills taught in school.
- Marking grids are included to record results for these units.

Unit C: Focus on problem solving

- This unit covers all the strands of the Mathematics Curriculum: Number, Algebra, Measurement, Space, Statistics and Probability.
- Each unit consists of nine problem-style questions for students to solve.
- This unit is written in themes with real-life problems to solve. Themes provide a context for the mathematics questions and make mathematical problem-solving more relevant to students.

Unit D: Focus on challenge

- The format varies from unit to unit because the questions draw from the different strands of the Mathematics Curriculum and therefore require more demanding higher-order thinking skills to solve.
- This unit is designed to help students develop deeper understandings about mathematical concepts.
- This unit is also written in themes with real-life problems to provide a challenge for students.

NAPLAN-style tests

- Two four-page NAPLAN-style tests provide early practice in taking tests.

Answers

- Answer pages provide answers for each question.

Introduction

Important note about Unit C: Focus on problem solving and Unit D: Focus on challenge

Parents and teachers please note that the questions in Units C and D require an advanced level of skill in English reading and comprehension. Students with advanced ability in mathematics will not necessarily also have advanced ability in English so these students might need adult (or other competent reader) support for the reading in these parts. Please read the questions for students if they experience difficulty with the reading.

How to use this book with the *Excel* Advanced Skills: Advanced English series

For a complete weekly English and Mathematics program use this book in conjunction with the ***Excel*** Advanced Skills: Advanced English Year 2 book. This way a student will have work set for four days a week: two days for English and two days for Mathematics.

How to assess students' progress

The results of the work undertaken in Units A and B can be recorded on the marking grids. The marking grids on pages 8 and 9 (please see the example on page 6) are easy-to-use diagnostic tools that indicate where students' strengths and weaknesses lie in relation to specific areas of Mathematics. These results can be used to gather extra information about students' progress and their further revision needs.

The *Excel* Basic and Advanced Skills series

If students are experiencing difficulty, require additional practice or need extension in any area of the course, further books are available to support them in the ***Excel*** Basic Skills and Advanced Skills series. Please see the comprehensive list of ***Excel*** books on page 7.

The *Excel* step-by-step improvement plan

Step 1

Read the introduction on pages 4–5.

Step 2

The results of the work undertaken in Units A and B can be recorded on the marking grids provided.

This is an easy-to-use diagnostic tool that indicates both where each student's strengths and weaknesses are in relation to specific areas of Mathematics as well as their ability to work at different levels of difficulty.

These results can be used to gather extra information about each student's progress and their further revision needs.

When marking answers on the grids, simply mark incorrect answers with 'X' in the appropriate box. This will result in a graphical representation of areas needing further work.

If a student is consistently getting more than one in five questions wrong in any topic, they need help in this area.

Five questions of a sample marking grid are shown below. If a question has several parts, it should be counted as wrong if one or more mistakes are made.

	Division	Division	Fractions	Money	Money
Questions	**1**	**2**	**3**	**4**	**5**
Unit 1B					
Unit 2B					X
Unit 3B					
Unit 4B					X
Unit 5B					
Unit 6B					X
Unit 7B					
Unit 8B					X
Unit 9B					
Unit 10B					X

This grid indicates that the student needs extra help and practice with questions on money.

Step 3

Refer to page 7: *Excel* books to help you *get the results you want*!

Under each topic there is a comprehensive list of books in our range to help students practise the topic they are having difficulty with.

For example, if a student wants more practice with subtraction questions, the books shown will help them. Each ***Excel*** book has a comprehensive contents page that will identify the appropriate pages in the book to target the specific topic area that is causing problems.

Excel books to help you *get the results you want!*

NUMBER AND ALGEBRA

	Excel Basic Skills			*Excel* Advanced Skills	*Excel* NAPLAN-style Tests		
Place value; patterns and sequences	 9781864413397	 9781741257113	 9781741251852	 9781741254631	 9781741254389	 9781741254099	 9781741254198
Addition; subtraction	 9781864412864	 9781741257113	 9781741251852	 9781741254631	 9781741254389	 9781741254099	 9781741254198
Multiplication; division	 9781864412888	 9781740200295	 9781741257113	 9781741254631	 9781741254389	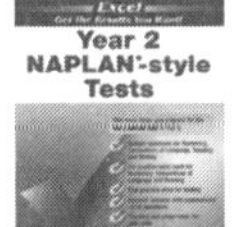 9781741254099	 9781741254198
Fractions; money	  9781741255881	 9781741257113	 9781741251852	 9781741254631	  9781741254389	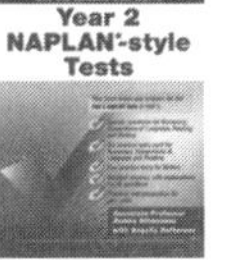 9781741254099	 9781741254198

MEASUREMENT AND SPACE

	Excel Basic Skills			*Excel* Advanced Skills	*Excel* NAPLAN-style Tests		
Time; measurement	 9781741255881	 9781741257113	  9781741251852	 9781741254631	  9781741254389	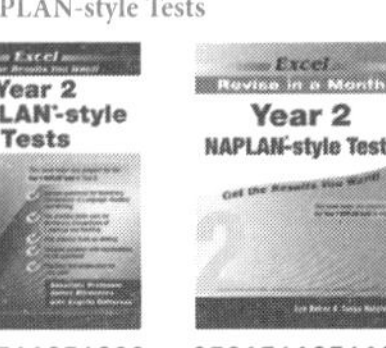 9781741254099	9781741254198
2D and 3D shapes; location; transformation	 9781741256178	 9781741257113	 9781741251852	 9781741254631	 9781741254389	 9781741254099	 9781741254198

STATISTICS AND PROBABILITY

	Excel Basic Skills			*Excel* Advanced Skills	*Excel* NAPLAN-style Tests		
Statistics and probability	 9781741256178	 9781741257113	9781741251852	9781741254631	 9781741254389	 9781741254099	 9781741254198

Unit A marking grid

	Place value				Patterns and sequences		Addition			Subtraction			Multiplication	
Questions	1	2	3	4	5	6	7	8	9	10	11	12	13	14
Unit 1A														
Unit 2A														
Unit 3A														
Unit 4A														
Unit 5A														
Unit 6A														
Unit 7A														
Unit 8A														
Unit 9A														
Unit 10A														
Unit 11A														
Unit 12A														
Unit 13A														
Unit 14A														
Unit 15A														
Unit 16A														
Unit 17A														
Unit 18A														
Unit 19A														
Unit 20A														
Unit 21A														
Unit 22A														
Unit 23A														
Unit 24A														
Unit 25A														
Unit 26A														
Unit 27A														
Unit 28A														
Unit 29A														
Unit 30A														
Questions	1	2	3	4	5	6	7	8	9	10	11	12	13	14

Unit B marking grid

Questions	Division 1	Division 2	Fractions 3	Money 4	Money 5	Time 6	Time 7	Measurement 8	Measurement 9	2D and 3D shapes 10	2D and 3D shapes 11	Location 12	Transformation 13	Statistics and probability 14
Unit 1B														
Unit 2B														
Unit 3B														
Unit 4B														
Unit 5B														
Unit 6B														
Unit 7B														
Unit 8B														
Unit 9B														
Unit 10B														
Unit 11B														
Unit 12B														
Unit 13B														
Unit 14B														
Unit 15B														
Unit 16B														
Unit 17B														
Unit 18B														
Unit 19B														
Unit 20B														
Unit 21B														
Unit 22B														
Unit 23B														
Unit 24B														
Unit 25B														
Unit 26B														
Unit 27B														
Unit 28B														
Unit 29B														
Unit 30B														
Questions	1	2	3	4	5	6	7	8	9	10	11	12	13	14

NUMBER AND ALGEBRA

1 Expand the numbers.

23 = ☐ tens ☐ ones

31 = ☐ tens ☐ ones

2 Which number is largest? ☐

A 48 B 84 C 44 D 64

3 What is one hundred and nineteen written as a number? ☐

A 911 B 190 C 119 D 191

4

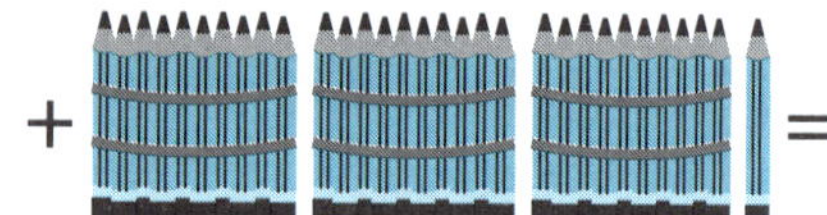

+ 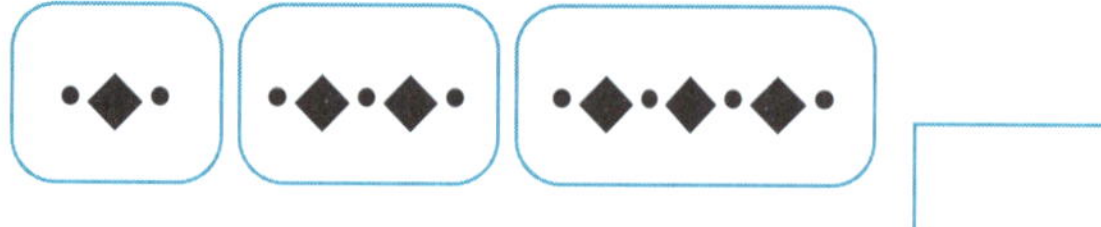 =

☐

5 0, 5, 10, 15

What number is being added each time?

☐

6 What pattern will be on the next card?

•◆• | •◆•◆• | •◆•◆•◆•

☐

A •◆• B •◆•◆•

C ◆•◆•◆•◆ D •◆•◆•◆•◆•

7

2 + 8 = 3 + ☐

8 Complete the table.

+	20	21	22	23
3				

9 Which is the same as 8 + 5? ☐

A 5 + 8 B 8 + 6 C 6 + 8 D 7 + 6

10 Complete the table.

–	10	15	20	25
5				

11 Draw an arrow on the number line to show starting at 10 and counting back 2.

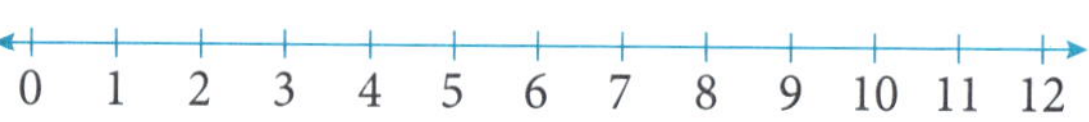

Where do you land? ☐

A 10 B 9 C 8 D 2

12 What is the difference between 20 and 30? ☐

13 Circle three groups of three.

14 How should you write **3 groups of 3** as a number sentence? ☐

A 3 + 3 + 3 + 3 B 3 ÷ 3

C 9 – 3 D 3 × 3

NUMBER AND ALGEBRA

1 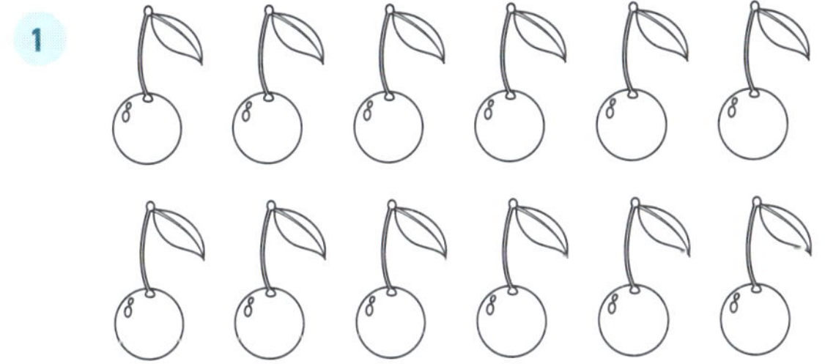

Circle the cherries in groups of two. How many groups are there?

2 Share 10 strawberries between 2 children. How many strawberries will each child get?

3 Choose the two circles that have been cut into halves.

A B C D

4 Circle coins to make $2.50.

 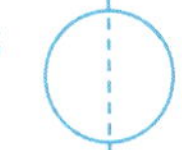   

5 Circle each coin that is worth less than 50c.

MEASUREMENT AND SPACE

6     

02:30

The time is half past ________.

7 Draw hands on the clock to show half past two.

8 Name the month that follows June.

9 Colour the container to show that it is half full.

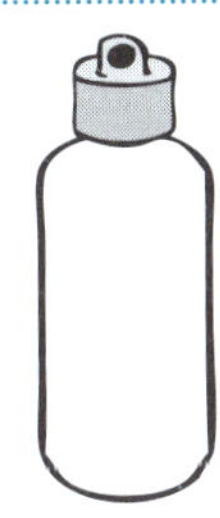

10 Colour the triangles.

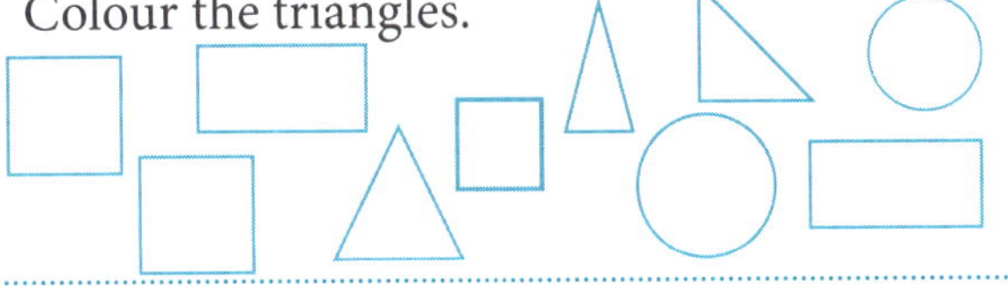

11 Circle the objects that will roll.

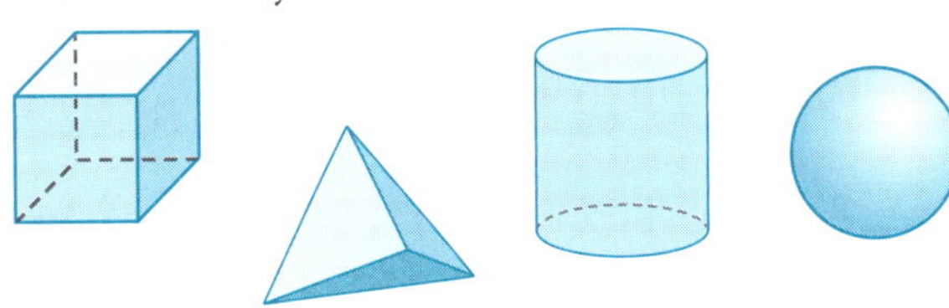

12 Draw a star at B2.

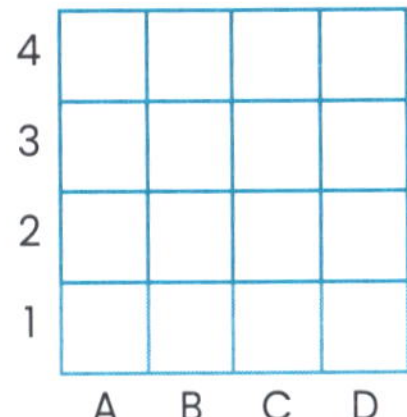

13 Here is an arrow. 
What does it look like after a half turn clockwise?

A B C D

STATISTICS AND PROBABILITY

14 Which vegetable is most popular?

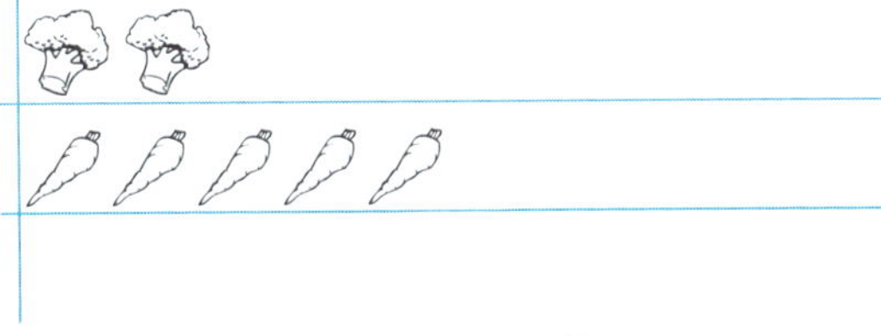

A  B 
C 

Meet Sasha

Show your working out in number sentences or drawings.

NUMBER AND ALGEBRA

1. Sasha invited twelve people to her party. They all said yes but Sam got sick and could not come. Then Vicky asked if she could bring her cousin and Sasha said yes. How many people came to the party?

2. Nana cooked 12 cupcakes for the party. Pop cooked 10 scones. How many items did they make altogether?

3. Sasha ate 10 cherries. Jaala ate 7 more than her. How many did Jaala eat?

4. Help Sasha share the chocolate with 3 friends. How many squares will each child get?

5. Eighteen children in Sasha's class shared the use of six soccer balls. How many children had to share each ball?

   A $18 \div 6$ **B** $18 + 6$
   C $6 + 6 = 6 + 6 + 6$ **D** $18 - 6$

MEASUREMENT AND SPACE

6. Sasha's party started at 12 o'clock on Saturday. It finished 2 hours later. Draw the hands on the clock to show the time it finished.

7. Sasha needs help to make a cake. The recipe says she needs 100 ? sugar. Which measurement would be accurate?

   A 100 centimetres **B** 100 kilograms
   C 100 grams **D** 100 metres

8. Sasha used a broken ruler to measure the width of her hand. How wide is her hand?

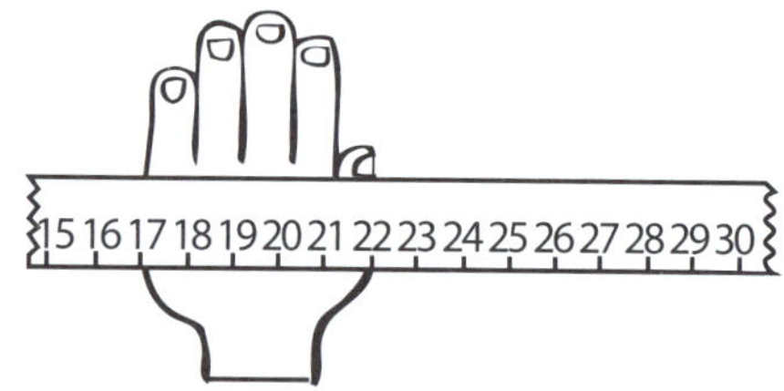

   A 17 centimetres **B** 22 centimetres
   C 5 centimetres **D** 7 centimetres

STATISTICS AND PROBABILITY

9. Dad has a bag of jelly beans. There are an equal number of five colours: red, yellow, green, orange and white. What is Sasha's chance of getting a red one if she selects one without looking?

   A likely **B** certain
   C unlikely **D** impossible

MEASUREMENT

10 Sasha drew three things she did yesterday.

a Estimate how long Sasha spent doing each activity and write your estimate on the line.

b Under each clock write the time in words.

Time spent on this activity ______________________

Eating breakfast

Time spent on this activity ______________________

In class doing maths

Time spent on this activity ______________________

At school gymnastics

11 **a** Draw three things you usually do during a 24-hour period. Draw one thing at home, one while you are at school and one activity in the community.

b Draw hands on the clocks to show the time at which you do each activity.

c Beside each drawing, write how long you spend doing the activity.

12 How much time do you usually spend sleeping in a 24-hour period? ______________________

NUMBER AND ALGEBRA

1 Expand the numbers.

18 = [ ] tens [ ] ones

26 = [ ] tens [ ] ones

2 Which number is largest? [ ]

A 51 B 49 C 59 D 45

3 Write the number four hundred and twenty-three.

[ ]

4

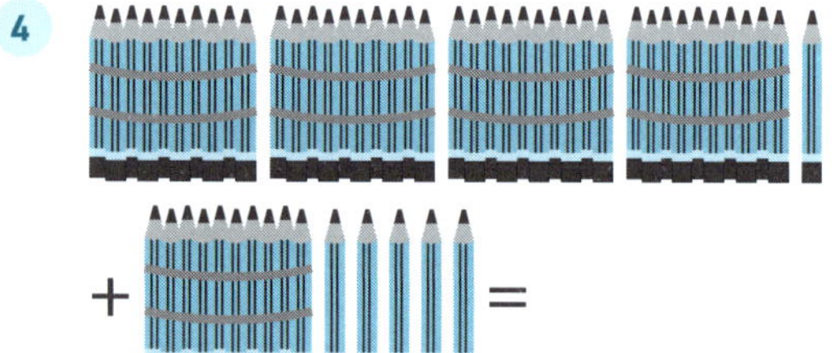

[ ]

5 50, 55, 60, 65
What number is being added in the pattern? [ ]

6

△	▲	
○	●	?
□		■

Which one belongs in the box with the [?]? [ ]

A  B   C  D 

7

4 + 6 = 5 + [ ]

8 Complete the table.

+	20	21	22	23
4				

9 Which is the same as 8 + 1? [ ]

A 8 + 8 B 16 + 8 C 1 + 8 D 1 + 9

10 Complete the table.

−	20	30	40	50
10				

11 Draw an arrow on the number line to show starting at 19 and counting back 4.

Where do you land? [ ]

A 14 B 23 C 16 D 15

12 What is the difference between 40 and 60? [ ]

13 Circle three groups of four.

☆ ☆ ☆
☆ ☆ ☆
☆ ☆ ☆
☆ ☆ ☆

14 How should you write **3 groups of 4**? [ ]

A 3 × 3 B 3 × 4
C 12 + 3 D 3 + 3 + 3 + 3

NUMBER AND ALGEBRA

1 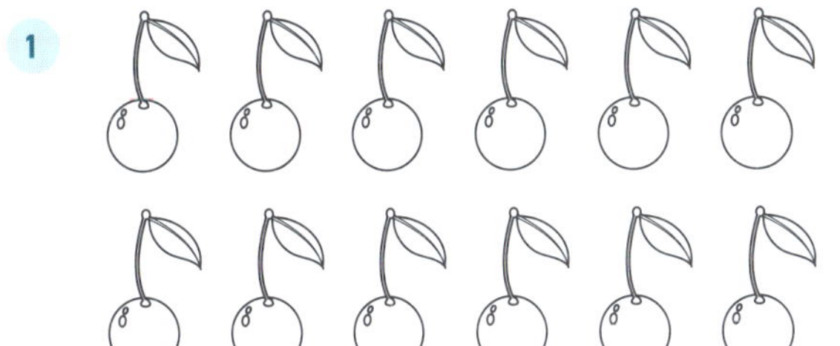

Circle the cherries in groups of three.
How many groups are there?

2 Share 12 chocolates between 6 children.
How many chocolates will each child get?

3 What fraction is shaded?

A one-half B one whole
C one-quarter D two-quarters

4 Which option shows four dollars and ten cents?

A $4.10 B $450 C $4.00 D $410

5 Colour each coin that is worth more than 50c.

MEASUREMENT AND SPACE

6 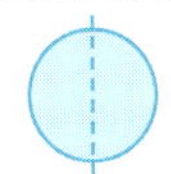

Write the time in words.

7 Draw hands on the clock to show half past four.

8 Name the month that follows October.

9 Which container holds the most?

A 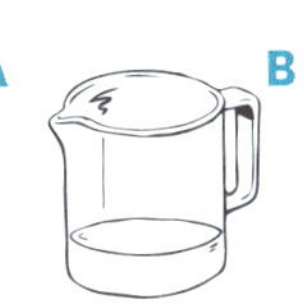 B  C  D 

10 Colour the shapes that have four corners.

11 Which object has the most faces?

A  B 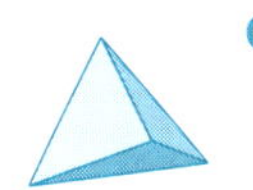 C  D 

12 Draw a circle at C4.

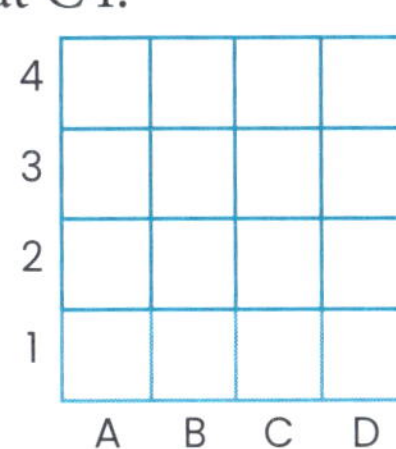

13 Here is an arrow. 
What does it look like after a quarter turn anticlockwise?

A  B  C  D 

STATISTICS AND PROBABILITY

14 Which vegetable is least popular?

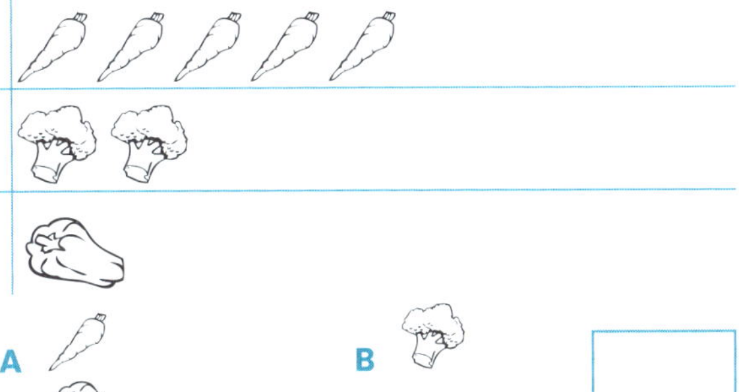

NUMBER AND ALGEBRA

1 Expand the numbers.

42 = [ ] tens [ ] ones

34 = [ ] tens [ ] ones

2 Which number is largest? [ ]

A 29 **B** 19 **C** 91 **D** 20

3 Write the number two hundred and sixteen.

[ ]

4

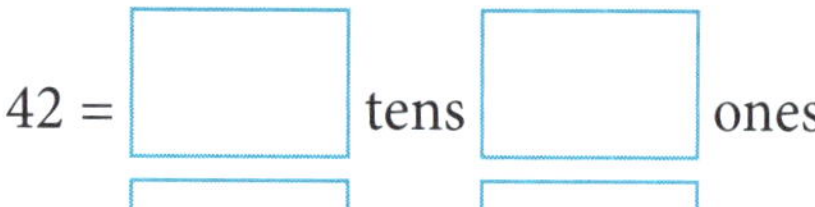

\+ 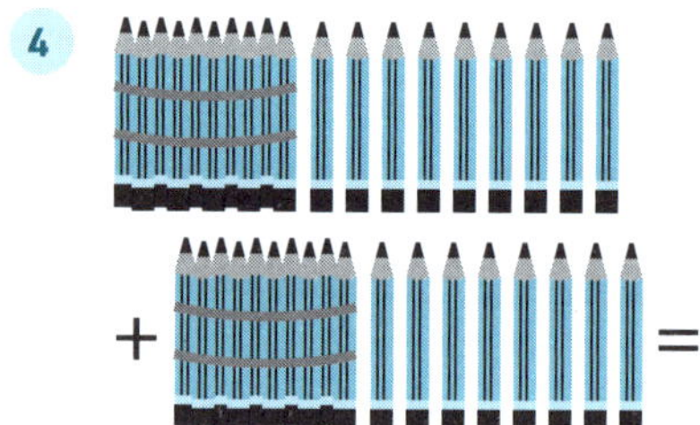 =

[ ]

5 50, 60, 70, 80
What number is being added in the pattern? [ ]

6

Which one belongs in the last box? [ ]

A  **B**  **C**  **D** 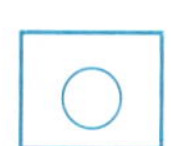 

7

3 + 7 = 1 + [ ]

8 Complete the table.

+	20	21	22	23
6				

9 Which is the same as 8 + 4? [ ]

A 4 + 8 **B** 8 + 14 **C** 14 **D** 7+ 7

10 Complete the table.

−	20	30	40	50
2				

11 Draw an arrow on the number line to show starting at 20 and counting back 5.

10 11 12 13 14 15 16 17 18 19 20 21 22

Where do you land? [ ]

A 14 **B** 17 **C** 16 **D** 15

12 What is the difference between 70 and 60? [ ]

13 Circle five groups of two.

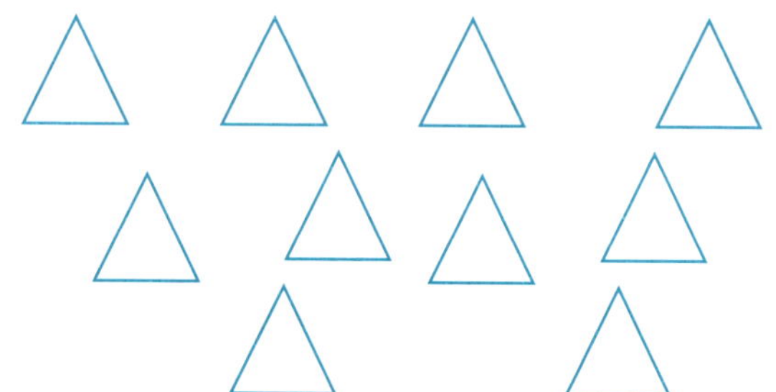

14 How should you write **5 groups of 2**? [ ]

A 2 + 2 + 2 + 2 **B** 5 + 2

C 5 + 5 **D** 5 × 2

NUMBER AND ALGEBRA

1 

Circle the strawberries in groups of three.
How many groups are there?

2 Share 12 books between 6 children.
How do you work out how many each child will get?

A 12 – 6 B 12 ÷ 6 C 12 ÷ 2 D 6 × 6

3 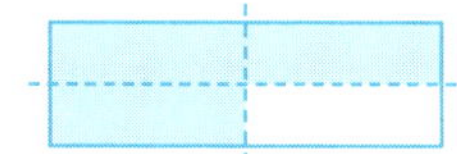

The fraction shaded is

A three-quarters. B one-half.

C one-quarter. D two-quarters.

4 Which option shows one dollar and ten cents?

A \$110 B \$10.1 C \$1.1 D \$1.10

5 Circle coins to make \$1.

MEASUREMENT AND SPACE

6 12:00 Write the time in words.

7 Draw hands on the clock to show half past six.

8 How many days are in September?

9 Eve's ribbon is

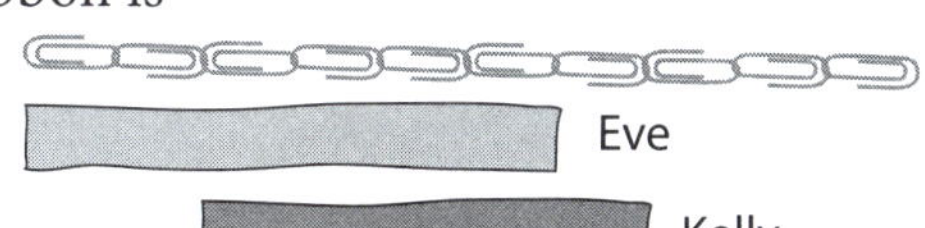

A shorter than B longer than

C the same length as

Kelly's ribbon.

10 Colour the rectangles.

11 Circle the object which has five corners.

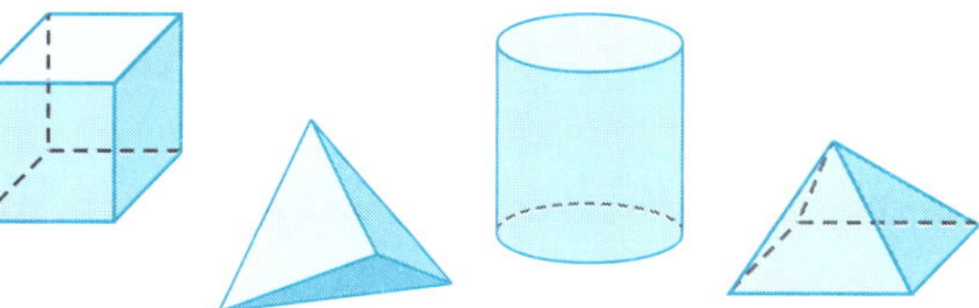

12 Draw a cross at C1 and a triangle at D4.

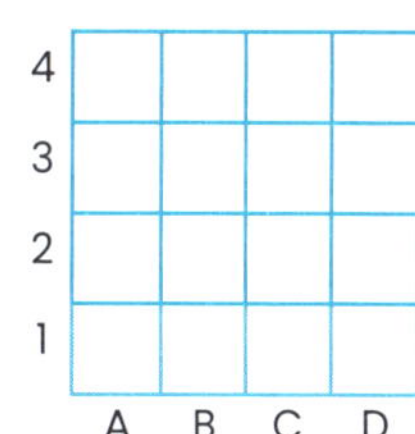

13 Here is an arrow.
Draw the arrow after a half turn anticlockwise.

STATISTICS AND PROBABILITY

14 Add two apples to the graph.

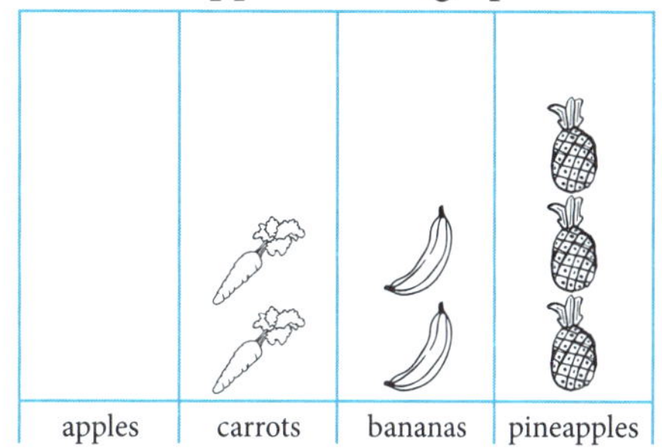

My name is Jin

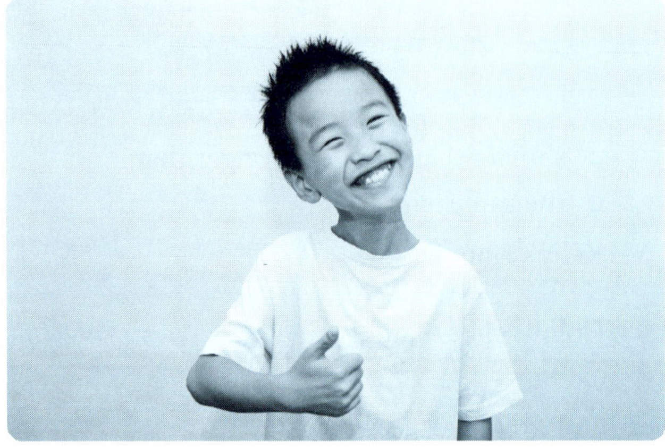

Show your working out in number sentences or drawings.

NUMBER AND ALGEBRA

1 Jin lives with five other people, a dog and five fish. How many beings live in Jin's home?

2 Jin's grandmother used to have 15 goldfish in her pond but a magpie ate two. How many are left?

3 Jin's sister is paid $10 to walk the neighbour's dog every Saturday. How much will she earn in 4 weeks?

4 Jin's mum ordered 3 pizzas. Each pizza had 8 slices. How many slices were there altogether?

5 Jin has saved $6 towards a new comic book that costs $12. What fraction of the amount has he saved so far?

A three-quarters B two-thirds
C one-half D one-quarter

MEASUREMENT AND SPACE

6 Dog food comes in 20-kilogram bags. Each bag lasts for four weeks. How much does the dog eat each week?

7 The dog likes to walk around the outside of the playground. The playground is a rectangle that is 300 metres by 200 metres. How far does she walk when she walks all the way around?

8 Jin has a dental appointment on Monday at half past four. It takes 30 minutes to drive to the dentist. What time will he need to leave home?

STATISTICS AND PROBABILITY

9 Jin has a bag of marbles. There are 15 green ones and 3 blue ones. If he selects one without looking, how likely is it he will select a green one?

A likely B unlikely
C certain D impossible

MEASUREMENT

MARCH						
Monday	Tuesday	Wednesday	Thursday	Friday	Saturday	Sunday
			1	2	3	4
5	6	7	8	9	10	11
12	13	14	15	16	17	18
19	20	21	22	23	24	25
26	27	28	29	30	31	

10 a Jin's birthday is 22 March. What day of the week is that? ______

b Jin will celebrate his birthday with friends on the Saturday after his birthday.

What date will that be? ______

c Jin's grandmother's birthday is five days after Jin's. What date is that? ______

d Jin has a dental appointment on 5 March at half past four. Mark it on the calendar.

e Jin's sister has Little Athletics every Wednesday and Friday.

How many times will she go during March? ______

f Jin's class has library on Thursdays. Draw red stripes on the Thursdays on the calendar.

g It rained for four days from 2 March. Colour the rainy days blue.

11 What day of the week is 4 April?

______

12 What day of the week was the last day of February?

______

NUMBER AND ALGEBRA

1 Expand the numbers.

 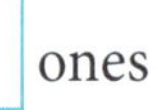

67 = ☐ tens ☐ ones

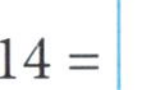

14 = ☐ tens ☐ ones

2 Which number is smallest? ☐

A 77 **B** 17 **C** 71 **D** 7

3 Write the number six hundred and five.

☐

4

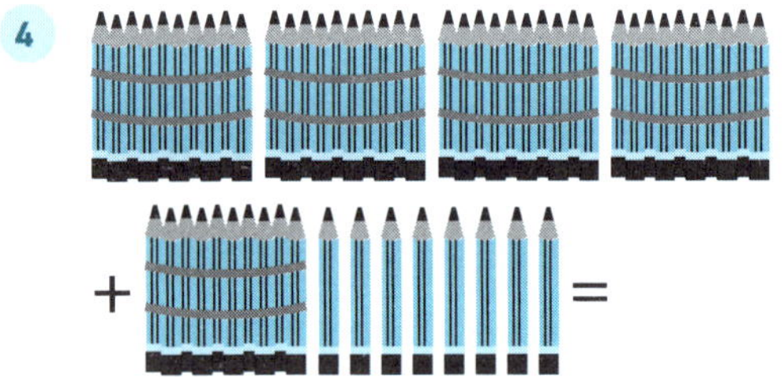

☐

5 12, 15, 18, 21
What number is being added in this pattern? ☐

6

Which one belongs in the empty box? ☐

A   **B**   **C** 

7 21 + 19 has the same value as ☐

A 22 + 20 **B** 30 + 20
C 20 + 20 **D** 30 + 9

8 Complete the table.

+	13	23	33	43
7				

9 Which is the same as 19 + 1? ☐

A 1 + 20 **B** 1 + 19 **C** 19 **D** 19 + 2

10 Complete the table.

−	25	35	45	55
2				

11 Draw an arrow on the number line to show starting at 45 and counting back 5.

Where do you land? ☐

A 45 **B** 50 **C** 55 **D** 40

12 What is the difference between 80 and 30? ☐

13 Circle two groups of three birds.

14 Which one says **2 groups of 3**? ☐

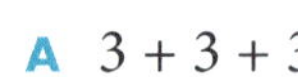

A 3 + 3 + 3 **B** 2 × 3
C 2 + 2 **D** 3 × 3

NUMBER AND ALGEBRA

1 Divide 16 by 4 using arrows to jump along the number line.

0 1 2 3 4 5 6 7 8 9 10 11 12 13 14 15 **16** 17 18 19 20

16 ÷ 4 = ☐

2 If you share 8 chocolates between 2 children, each child will get ☐ chocolates.

3 Colour three-quarters of the shape.

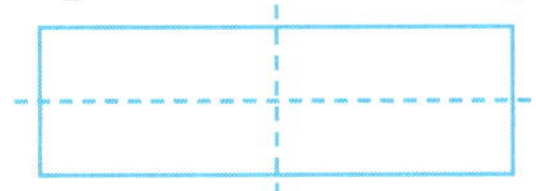

4 Which option shows three dollars and ten cents? ☐

A \$3.10 **B** \$30.10 **C** \$31.0 **D** \$30.1

5 Circle coins to make \$2.00.

MEASUREMENT AND SPACE

6 01:30 Write the time in words.

☐

7 Draw hands on the clock to show half past five.

8 Name the month before January.

☐

9 Jane is very thirsty. Which glass should she choose? ☐

A **B** **C**

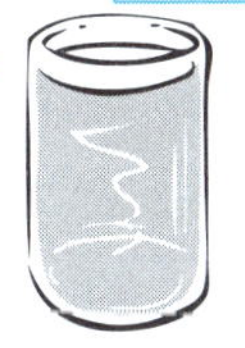

10 Colour the squares.

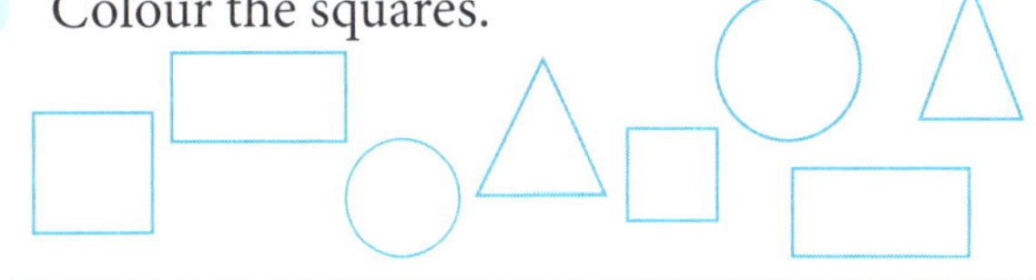

11 Circle the object that has no corners.

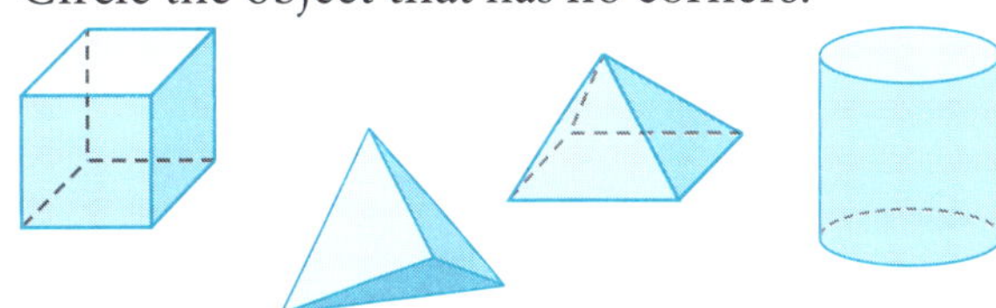

12 Draw flowers at C1 and A1.

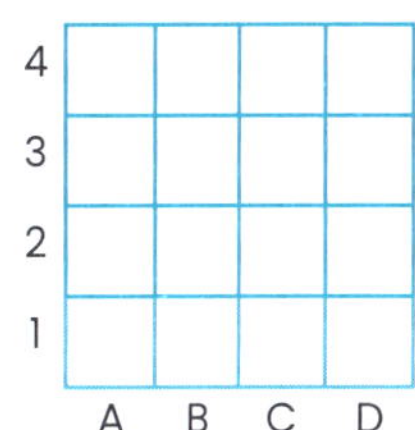

13 Here is an arrow. Draw the arrow after a half turn anticlockwise.

STATISTICS AND PROBABILITY

14 Add three apples to the graph.

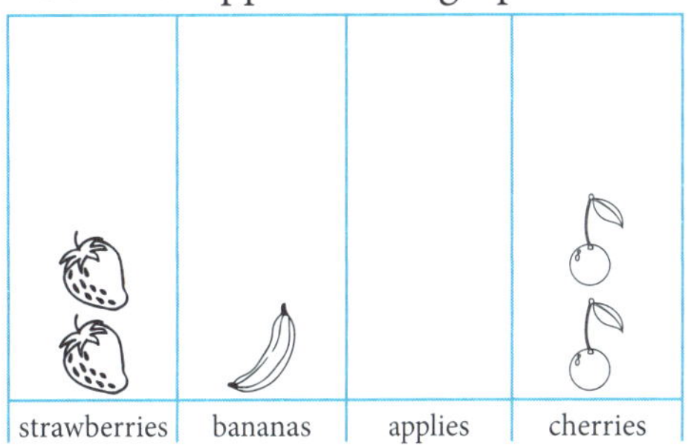

How many pieces of fruit did children bring to school? ☐

NUMBER AND ALGEBRA

1 Expand the numbers.

92 = ☐ tens ☐ ones

87 = ☐ tens ☐ ones

2 Which number is smallest? ☐

A 23 B 32 C 13 D 22

3 Write the number four hundred and fifteen.

☐

4

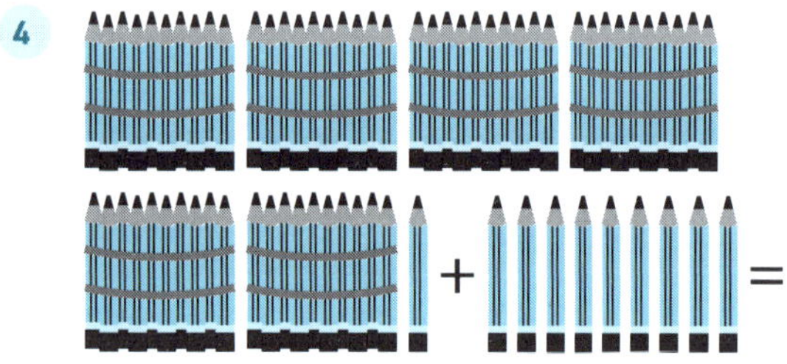

☐

5 24, 22, 20, 18

What number is being subtracted in the pattern? ☐

6 What shape belongs where the [?] is?

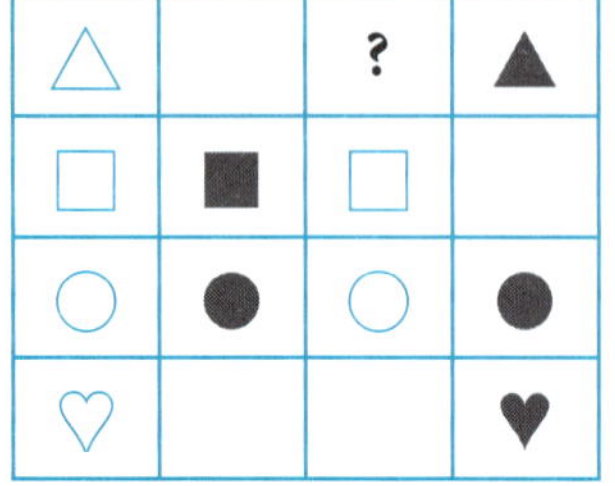

☐

A   B 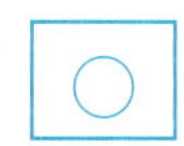  C  D 

7

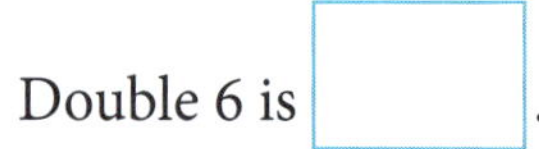

Double 6 is ☐.

8 Complete the table.

+	12	22	32	42
8				

9 Which is the same as 28 + 12? ☐

A 12 + 28 B 20 + 8

C 130 D 19 + 20

10 Complete the table.

–	10	20	30	40
4				

11 Draw an arrow on the number line to show starting at 23 and counting back 4.

Where do you land? ☐

A 14 B 17

C 16 D 19

12 What is the difference between 90 and 20? ☐

13 What is twice as much as five?

14 Which one says **2 groups of 4**? ☐

A 4×4

B $2 + 2 + 4$

C 2×4

D $2 + 4$

NUMBER AND ALGEBRA

1 Circle the stars in groups of 3.

18 ÷ 3 = ☐

2 Share 24 flowers between 2 teachers. How many will each teacher get?

24 ÷ 2 = ☐

3 Colour one-half of the flowers. ☐

The fraction coloured is

A $\frac{1}{5}$ B $\frac{1}{2}$ C $\frac{1}{4}$ D $\frac{1}{3}$

4 Which option shows five dollars and ninety cents? ☐

A 5.09 B $50.90 C $5.90 D $590

5 Circle coins to make $2.20.

   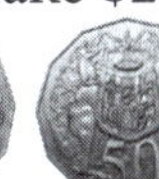    

MEASUREMENT AND SPACE

6 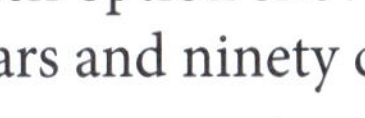

Write the time in words.

7 Draw hands on the clock to show half past eleven.

8 How many days are in December?

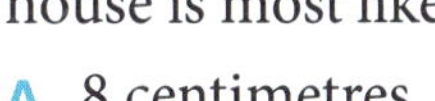

9 The height of a person's house is most likely ☐

A 8 centimetres. B 8 millimetres.

C 8 metres. D 8 kilometres.

10 Colour the circles.

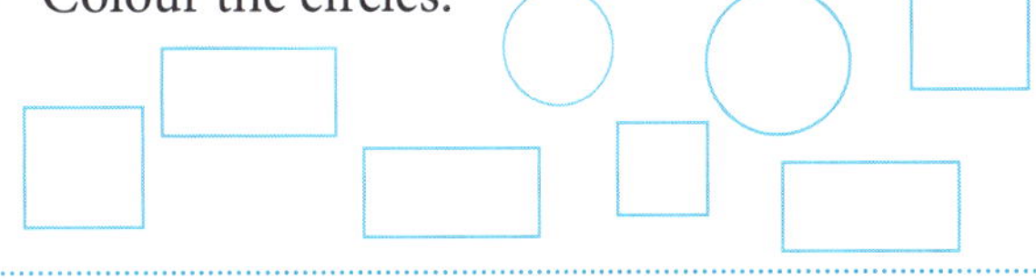

11 Colour the objects that will stack.

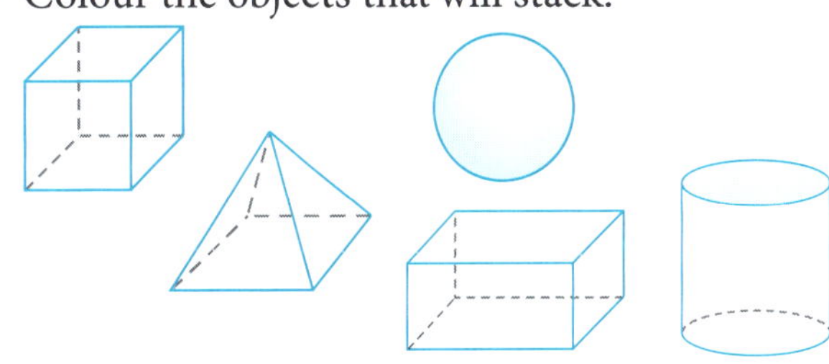

12 Draw a house in the position A1 and a sun at D4.

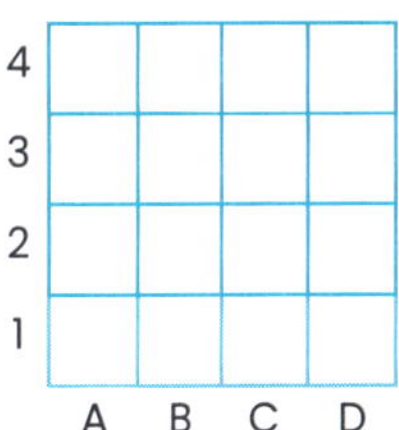

13 Draw the last box.

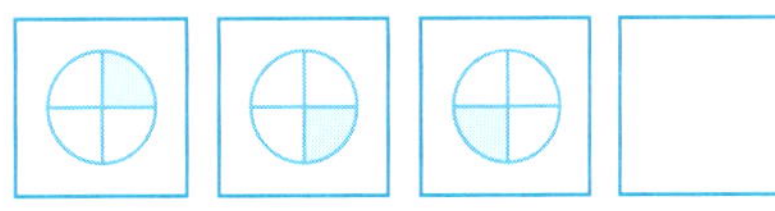

STATISTICS AND PROBABILITY

14 Children voted for their scariest animal.

Scary animals

elephants | tigers | snakes | spiders

Which animal is the scariest on the graph? ☐

Friends

Show your working out in number sentences or drawings.

NUMBER AND ALGEBRA

1 The shop sells muffins in packets of four. Ben needs 13 muffins for his soccer team. How many packets will he need to buy?

2 Between them, Ben and Matt have 30 marbles. If Matt owns 21 of them, how many does Ben own?

3 Ben and Matt are playing a maths game. It's Ben's turn. Help him choose two cards to make the number sentence correct.

☐ × ☐ = 20

5	12	7	3	4	6

4 There are five reading groups in Ben's class. Four groups have five children. One group has four children. How many children is that altogether? Which number sentence will help work out the answer?

A 5×5 B $5 \times 4 + 5$
C $4 \times 5 + 4$ D $5 \times 5 - 4$

5 Matt had 17 toffees that he and 4 friends shared fairly between them.

a How many toffees did they each get?

b How many toffees were left over?

MEASUREMENT AND SPACE

6 Ben needs to be at Matt's home at two o'clock. It's half past twelve now. How long before Ben needs to be there?

7 Ben and Matt designed a robot that they would build using recycled materials. How many rectangular prisms will they need?

8 It is 1 kilometre to Matt's home from Ben's. If Ben walks at 6 km per hour, how long will it take him to walk to Matt's?

A 6 hours B 10 minutes
C 60 minutes D 3 minutes

STATISTICS AND PROBABILITY

9 The weather report says there's a good chance it will rain in the afternoon. Should Ben take a raincoat when he walks to Matt's?

MEASUREMENT AND SPACE

10 This is a map of the area where Ben and Matt live. Draw the quickest route from Ben's to Matt's. Write instructions to tell someone the way. Use spare paper.

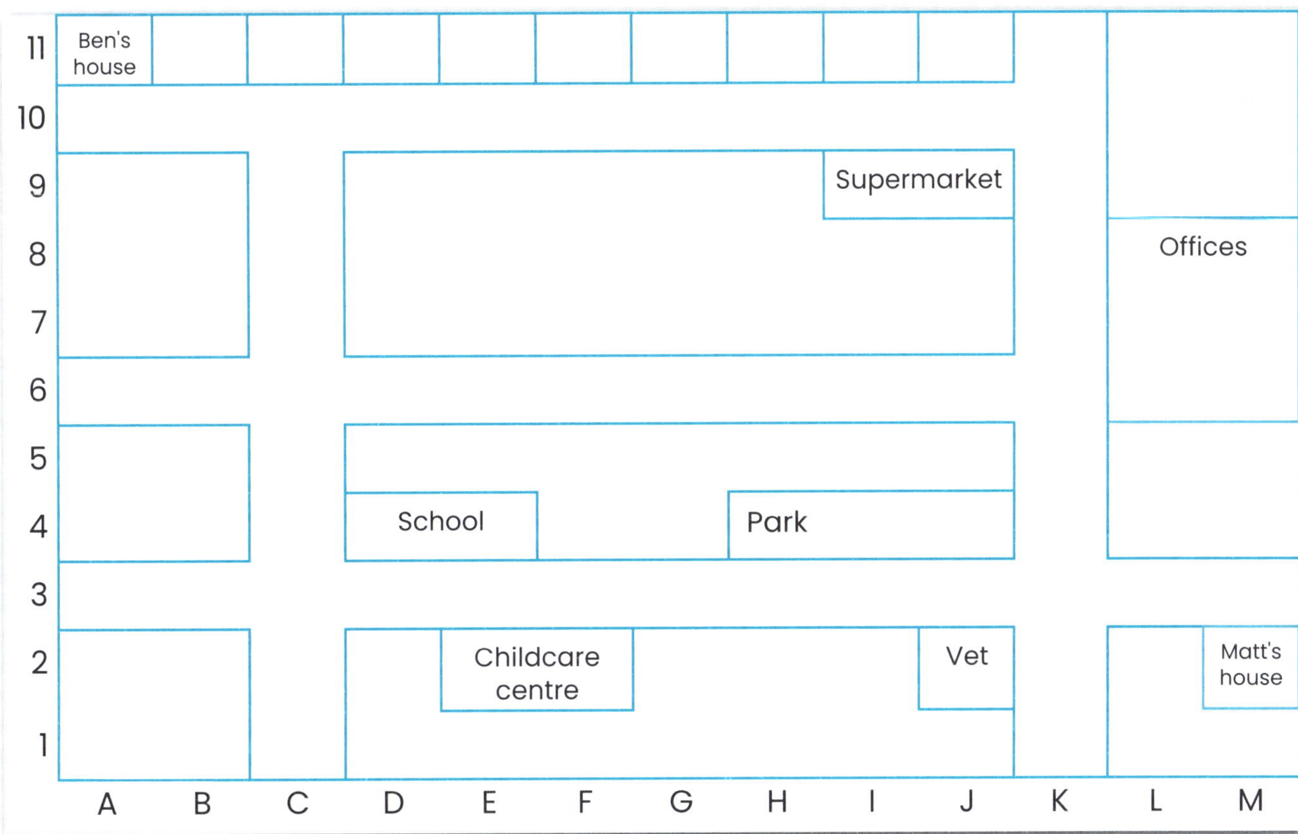

11 What is located at the following points on the map?

a M2 ____________________

b I9 ____________________

c E4 ____________________

d L8 ____________________

e H4 ____________________

f J2 ____________________

g E2 ____________________

12 Draw the following on the map:

a doctor's surgery at G11

b dentist at J7

c chemist at H11

d Zoe's house at B5

NUMBER AND ALGEBRA

1 Expand the numbers.

22 = ☐ tens ☐ ones

57 = ☐ tens ☐ ones

2 Which number is smallest?

A 65 B 56

C 60 D 50

☐

3 Write the number nine hundred and ten.

☐

4

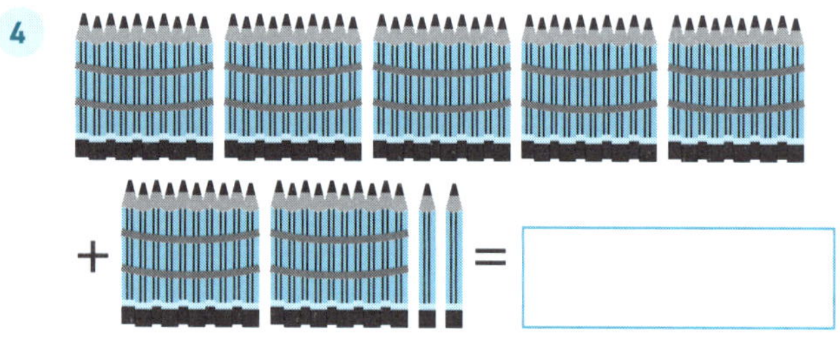

= ☐

5 2, 4, 6, 8

What number is being added in this pattern? ☐

6 Finish the pattern.

■●◆●■● ☐ ☐ ☐

7

Double 11 is ☐

8 Complete the table.

+	36	46	56	66
4				

9

18 + 5 has the same value as

20 + ☐

10 Complete the table.

–	10	20	30	40
6				

11 Draw an arrow on the number line to show starting at 30 and counting back 4.

20 21 22 23 24 25 26 27 28 29 30 31

Where do you land? ☐

A 24 B 25 C 26 D 27

12 What is the difference between 90 and 40? ☐

13 Draw five groups of three squares.

14 Four groups of three children is the same number of children as 2 groups of ☐

A 10 B 6

C 12 D 8

NUMBER AND ALGEBRA

1 Divide the stars into groups of 3.

21 ÷ 3 =

2 Share 24 flowers between 3 teachers. Which one helps work out how many flowers each teacher will get?

A 24 + 3 B 3 × 24 C 24 ÷ 3 D 24 – 3

3 Colour one-quarter of the flowers.

4 Which option shows five dollars and ninety cents?

A $5.09 B $50.90 C $5.90 D $590

5 Circle coins to make $2.50.

MEASUREMENT AND SPACE

6 04:30 Write the time in words.

7 Draw hands on the clock to show half past one.

8 Name the month before March.

9 How many more blocks will you need to balance the scales if the blocks each weigh 10 grams?

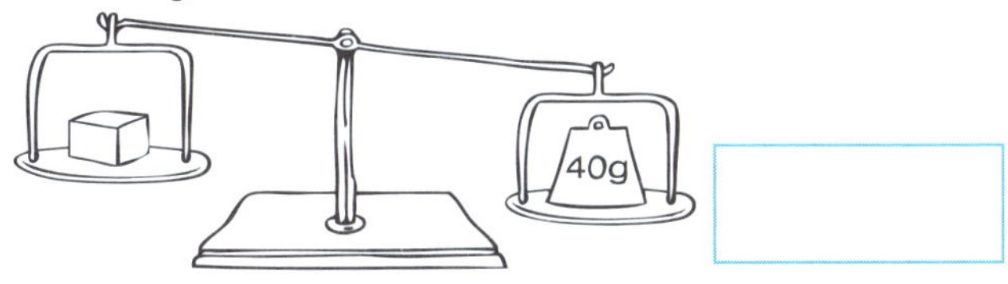

10 A square has four sides that are

A equal in length. B long.
C short. D different lengths.

11 Which object has six faces?

A 
B 

C 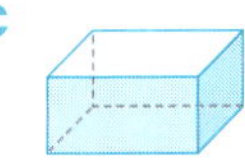
D 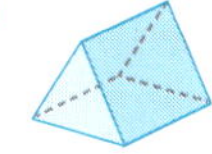

12 Draw spiders in B2 and C4.

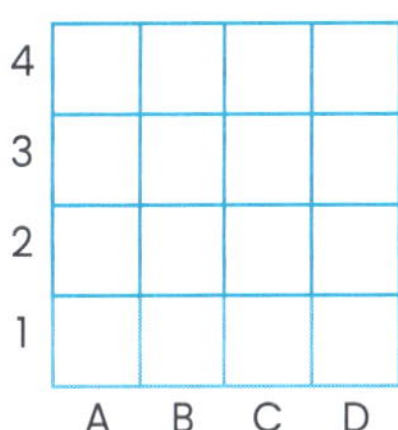

13 Draw the last box.

STATISTICS AND PROBABILITY

14 **Cutest animals**

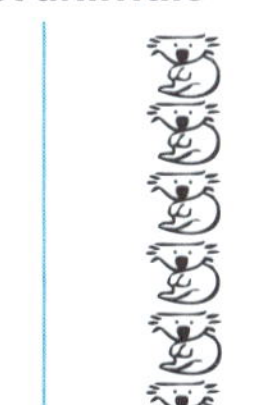

Which animal does the graph show is cutest?

NUMBER AND ALGEBRA

1

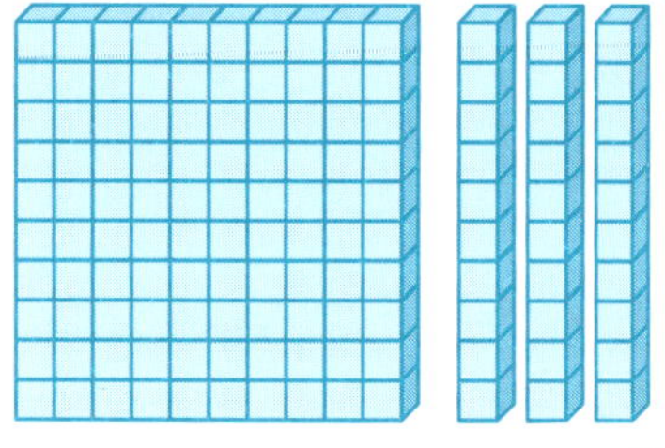

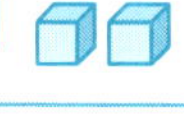

What is the number?

2 28, 18, 81

Write the numbers in sequence from smallest to largest.

3 Which number is closest to 19?

A 91 **B** seventeen

C 20 **D** twenty-one

4 What is the value of the hundreds digit in 486?

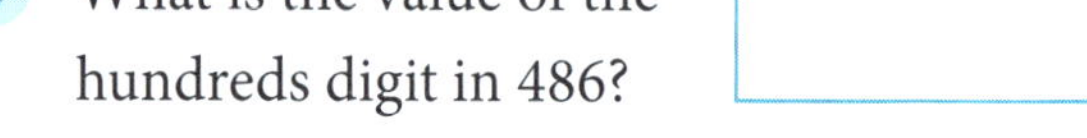

5 Write the next three numbers.

0, 5, 10, 15, ____, ____, ____

6 Finish the pattern.

7 Double 9 is ____.

8 Complete the table.

+	100	200	300	400
100				

9 Which has the same value as 18 + 5?

A 20 + 2 **B** 20 + 3

C 20 – 3 **D** 24

10

54 – 52 = ____

54 – ____ = 52

11 Draw an arrow on the number line to show starting at 20 and counting back 3.

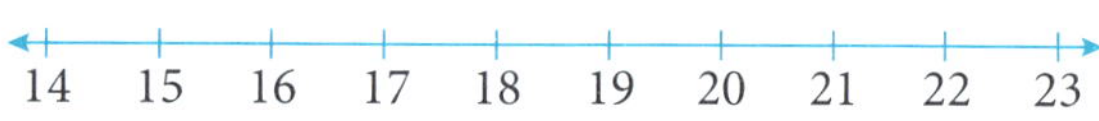

Write a number sentence to match.

12 Mum bought a box of 25 nails. She used 16. Which one helps work out how many were left?

A 25 + 16 **B** 25 – 16

C 9 + 25 **D** 25 ÷ 16

13 Draw three groups of three children. How many children are there?

14 Children worked in three groups of four to paint some murals. Which one helps you work out how many children were painting the murals?

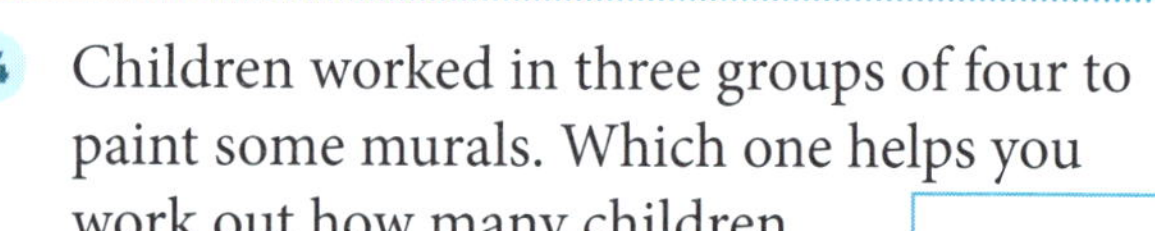

A 3 + 4 **B** 3 × 4

C 12 ÷ 3 **D** 12 – 4

NUMBER AND ALGEBRA

1 Circle pairs of socks.

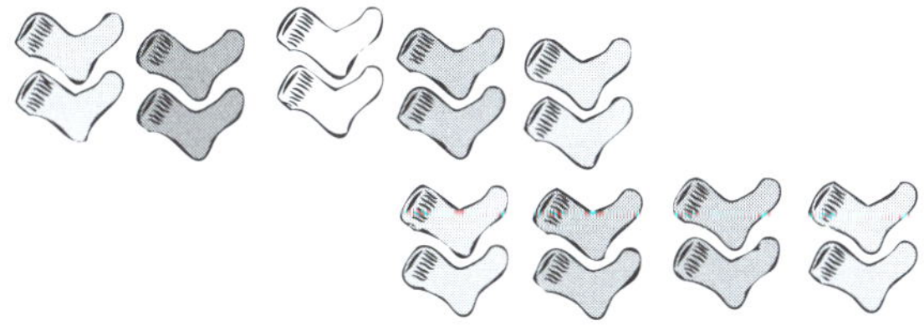

How many pairs are there?

2 Share 14 strawberries between 2 people. The number sentence is

A $14 \div 2 = 7$ B $14 + 2 = 16$

C $2 \times 14 = 28$ D $12 + 12 = 24$

3

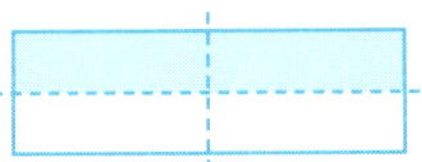

The fraction shaded is

A one-quarter. B one-eighth.

C one-third. D one-half.

4 What is the total value of the money?

5 Circle the coins Saskia should use to pay for an apple that costs 80c.

MEASUREMENT AND SPACE

6 10:30 Write the time in words.

7 Draw hands on the clock to show half past three.

8 What is the perimeter of the shaded rectangle? Remember that a perimeter is around the outside, like a fence.

9 If 5 March is a Sunday, what day is 7 March?

10 Which letter is in the square and the triangle but not the circle?

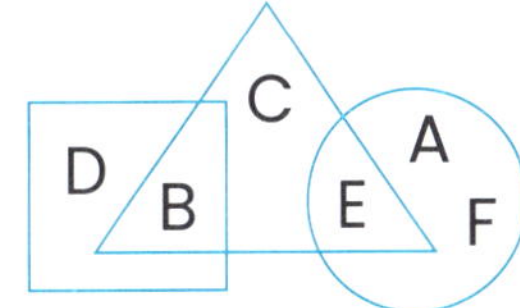

11 How many cubes are in the model?

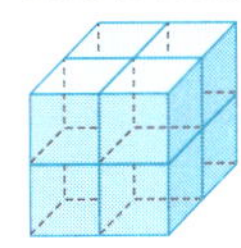

12 Circle the apple that is clockwise from the shaded apple.

13 Here is an arrow.

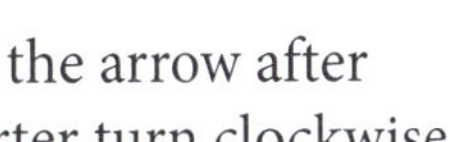

Draw the arrow after a quarter turn clockwise.

STATISTICS AND PROBABILITY

14 On which number is the spinner most likely to stop?

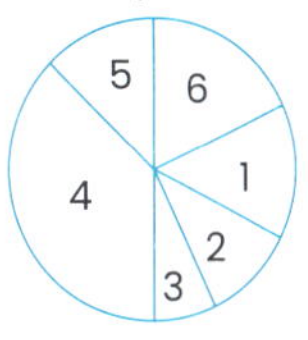

It's puzzling

Show your working out in number sentences or drawings.

NUMBER AND ALGEBRA

1. There are 15 boys in Year 2 who love doing jigsaw puzzles. The number of boys in the class who don't like puzzles is 5 more than those who do like them. How many boys don't like puzzles?

2. Jessica's jigsaw puzzle has 500 pieces. Todd's has 300 pieces. How many more pieces are in Jessica's puzzle?

3. Dad's jigsaw puzzle has 1000 pieces. He has almost half finished it. Approximately how many pieces does he have left to complete?

4. Which number sentence will give an answer of 6?

   A $1 + 2 \times 6$ **B** $1 \times 10 + 2$
   C $10 \div 2 + 1$ **D** $10 \div 1 + 2$

5. Jessica used the digits 2, 3 and 4 to make a number sentence where the answer is 14. What is the number sentence?

MEASUREMENT AND SPACE

6. Flynn took 1 hour to finish a jigsaw puzzle the first time he did it. He was 15 minutes faster the second time. How long did it take the second time?

7. Noah completed a jigsaw puzzle in one hour and fifteen minutes. He started at four o'clock. What time did he finish?

8. Sara took 45 minutes to complete a jigsaw puzzle. She finished at six o'clock. What time did she start?

STATISTICS AND PROBABILITY

9. A box contains 5 yellow marbles, 6 red marbles and 4 green marbles.

   Which colour is impossible to take from the box?

   A red **B** yellow
   C green **D** blue

NUMBER AND ALGEBRA

10 Maya is thinking of a number. Here are some clues so you can guess it.

It's less than 120 but more than 80. It has a 9 in the ones place.

The digit in the tens place is the same as the digit in the hundreds place.

What is Maya's number?

A 79 B 191 C 119 D 89

MEASUREMENT AND SPACE

11 A farmhouse has a window that looks like this from the outside. What does it look like from the inside?

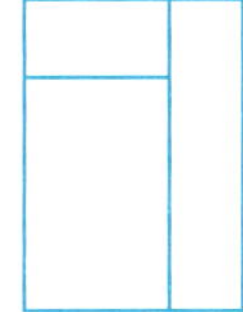

A 

B 

C 

D 

12 a Collect ten coins. Make a triangle of coins like the one pictured. Move only three coins to turn the triangle upside down.

b Get 11 popsticks or matchsticks. Make three squares as in the picture. Move three of the sticks to make two squares.

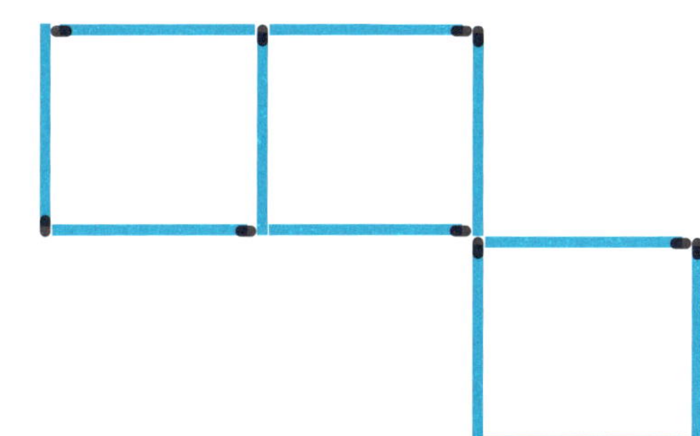

c Which piece is missing from the puzzle?

A 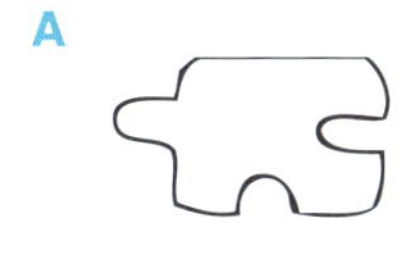

B 

C 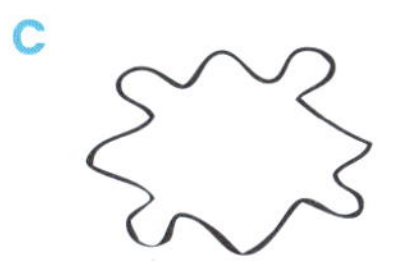

D 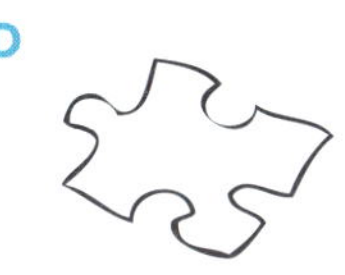

NUMBER AND ALGEBRA

1 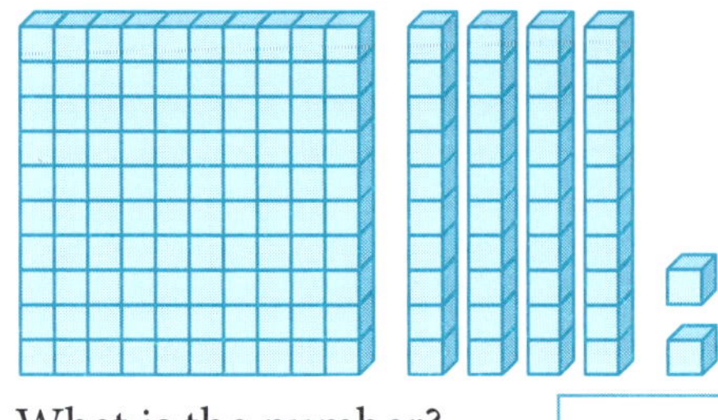

What is the number?

2 38, 83, 33

Write the numbers in sequence from smallest to largest.

3 Which number is closest to 21?

A 12 B sixteen
C twenty D 23

4 What is the value of the hundreds digit in 654?

5 25, 22, 19, 16
This pattern is going backwards by .

6 Draw the shape that comes next in the pattern.

7 Double 7 is 

8 Complete the table.

+	100	200	300	400
200				

9 Which is the same as 19 + 11?

A 11 + 9 B 20 + 0
C 20 + 10 D 19 + 10

10

65 – 5 =

65 – 60 =

11 Show 46 –7 on the number line. Write a number sentence to match the number line.

38 39 40 41 42 43 44 45 46 47 48

12 Jeremy had 20 marbles. He lost 3. How many were left?

13 Draw two groups of six children. How many children are there?

14 Some children worked in four groups of four. Which one helps you work out how many children there were altogether?

A 4 + 4 B 4 × 4 C 16 – 4 D 16 ÷ 4

NUMBER AND ALGEBRA

1 Share 28 cupcakes equally between 4 plates. Draw the cupcakes on the plates.

2 Lexi and Dave share 16 strawberries equally. How many will Dave get?

3 If the shapes are folded along the dotted lines, which shapes will fold into two equal halves?

A 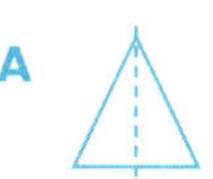

B 

C 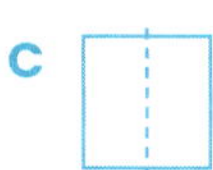

D 

4 Circle the two price tags that add up to $3.75.

5 Circle the coins Quan will use to pay for a mandarin that costs 55c.

MEASUREMENT AND SPACE

6 How many minutes are in one hour?

7 Draw hands on the clock to show 12:30.

8 How many months are in one year?

9 What is the perimeter of the shaded rectangle? Remember that the perimeter is around the outside, like a fence.

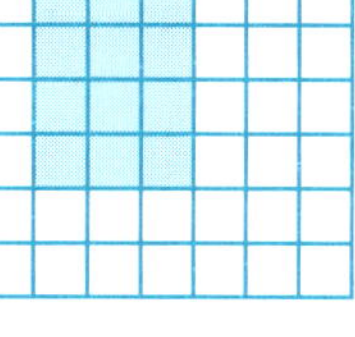

10 Colour the rectangles.

11 How many cubes are in this model?

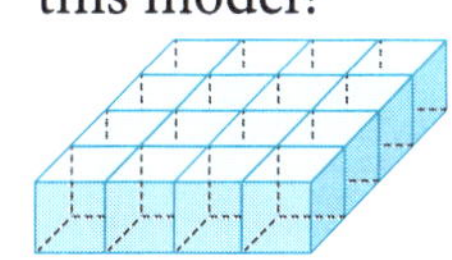

12 Circle the apple that is anticlockwise from the shaded apple.

13 Slide the rectangle 3 units up. Colour it in its new location.

STATISTICS AND PROBABILITY

14 On which number is the spinner **least likely** to stop?

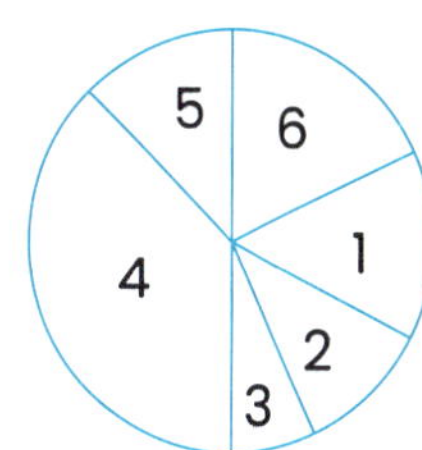

NUMBER AND ALGEBRA

1 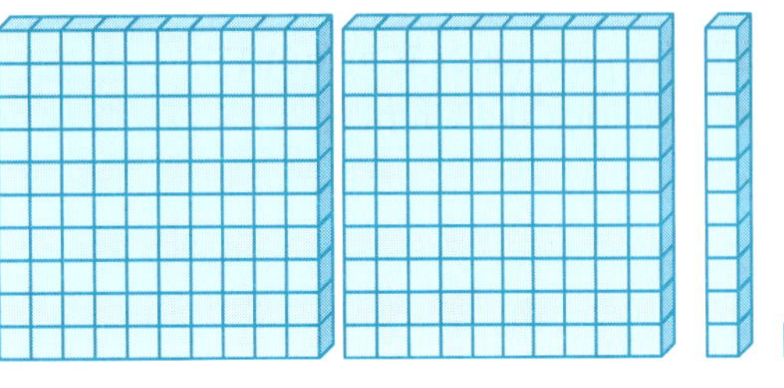

What is the number?

2 77, 17, 71

Write the numbers in sequence from smallest to largest.

3 Which number is closest to 42? 

A 52 B sixty-two

C forty D 45

4 What is the value of the hundreds digit in 506?

5 12, 14, 16, 18

What number is being added in the pattern? 

6 Draw the shape that comes next in the pattern.

7 Double 8 is

8 Complete the table.

+	100	200	300	400
300				

9 17 + 6 has the same value as

20 + ☐

10

25 − ☐ = 15

35 − ☐ = 25

11 Draw an arrow on the number line to show starting at 46 and going back 8.

36 37 38 39 40 41 42 43 44 45 46 47 48 49 50

Write a number sentence to match.

12 Tiffany had 30 marbles. She lost 11. How many did she have left?

13 Draw three groups of five children. How many children are there?

14 A reading class worked in five groups of five. Which one helps you work out how many children were in the class?

A 5 + 5 B 5 × 5

C 25 − 5 D 25 ÷ 5

NUMBER AND ALGEBRA

1 Divide 15 by 3 using arrows to jump along the number line.

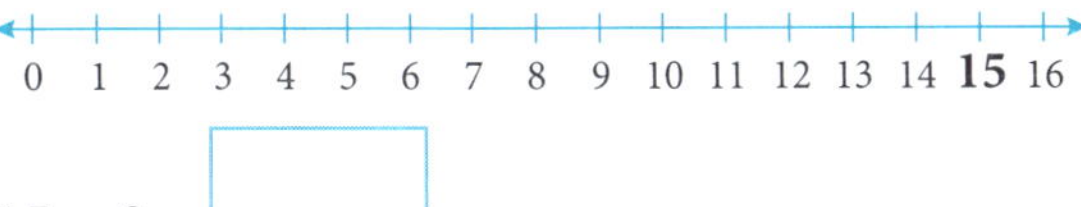

15 ÷ 3 = ☐

2 Share 16 pencils between 4 children. How many pencils will each child get? ☐

3

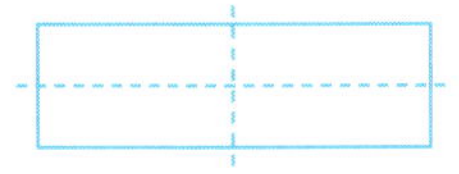

Colour one-quarter of the rectangle. ☐
The fraction coloured is

A $\frac{1}{5}$ **B** $\frac{1}{2}$ **C** $\frac{1}{4}$ **D** $\frac{1}{3}$

4 I have three dollars and thirty cents. Write the amount in numbers.

☐

5 Circle the coins Hung will use to pay for a sandwich that costs five dollars and twenty cents.

MEASUREMENT AND SPACE

6 09:30 Write the time in words.

☐

7 Draw hands on the clock to show 7:30.

8 How many hours are in one day?

9 What is the area of the shaded rectangle? Measure it in squares.

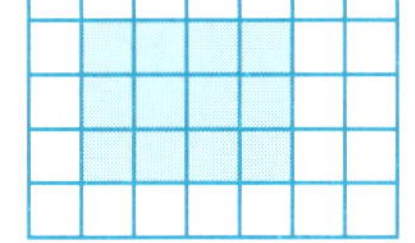

☐

10 Which descriptions are true?

A Opposite sides are the same length.

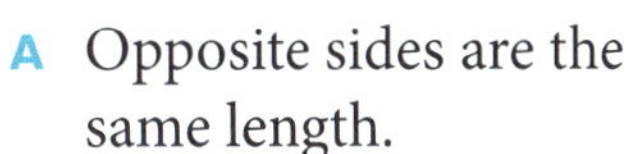

B Four sides are the same length.

C All angles are the same size.

D Only opposite angles are the same size.

E All sides are straight. ☐

11 Which object has no corners?

A 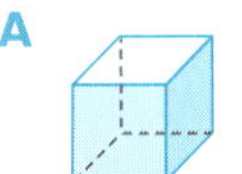 **B**   **C** 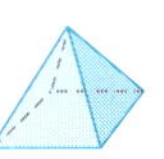 **D** 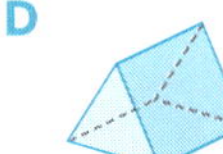

12 Circle the dog that is to the left of the shaded dog.

13 Here is an arrow. 

Draw the arrow after a quarter turn clockwise.

STATISTICS AND PROBABILITY

14 There are ten milk chocolates and two dark chocolates in a barrel.

Molly likes milk chocolate. What are her chances of getting a milk chocolate if she selects one without looking? ☐

A certain **B** likely

C unlikely **D** impossible

Animals are interesting

Show your working out in number sentences or drawings.

NUMBER AND ALGEBRA

1. A cat's brain weighs 30 g. An adult human brain weighs 1300 g. An elephant's brain weighs about 6 kg. Which brain is the heaviest?

2. Most spiders have eight eyes. How many more eyes does a spider have than a human?

3. An echidna can eat 200 g of ants in 10 minutes. 200 g of ants is about the same as
   - A a can of soup.
   - B a pumpkin.
   - C a cup of sugar.
   - D 1 paper clip.

4. Adult humpback whales can hold their breath for 40 minutes. Newborn humpbacks can hold their breath for 5 minutes. Which one helps work out how much longer an adult can hold its breath?
   - A $40 + 5$
   - B $40 \div 5$
   - C $40 + 40$
   - D $40 - 5$

5. A newborn humpback whale takes a breath every 5 minutes. Which one helps work out how many breaths they take in an hour?
   - A $60 \div 5$
   - B 5×60
   - C 1×5
   - D 5×15

MEASUREMENT AND SPACE

6. A rhinoceros beetle can lift 850 times its own body weight. A tiger can lift twice its body weight. Which is the stronger animal for its size?

7. A dog's eyeball is about 2 cm long. A colossal squid's eyeball is 23 cm long. The squid's eyeball is therefore about
   - A 10 times longer.
   - B 3 times longer.
   - C twice the size.
   - D 100 times longer.

8. Zander's cat eats $\frac{4}{5}$ of a cup of dried food a day. Colour the cup to show how much it eats.

STATISTICS AND PROBABILITY

9. Every night Mum and Ron toss a coin to see who will cook. Mum always tosses tails. Tails has won four nights in a row. Which result is more likely for the next toss?
   - A tails
   - B heads
   - C Heads and tails have the same chance.

MEASUREMENT AND SPACE

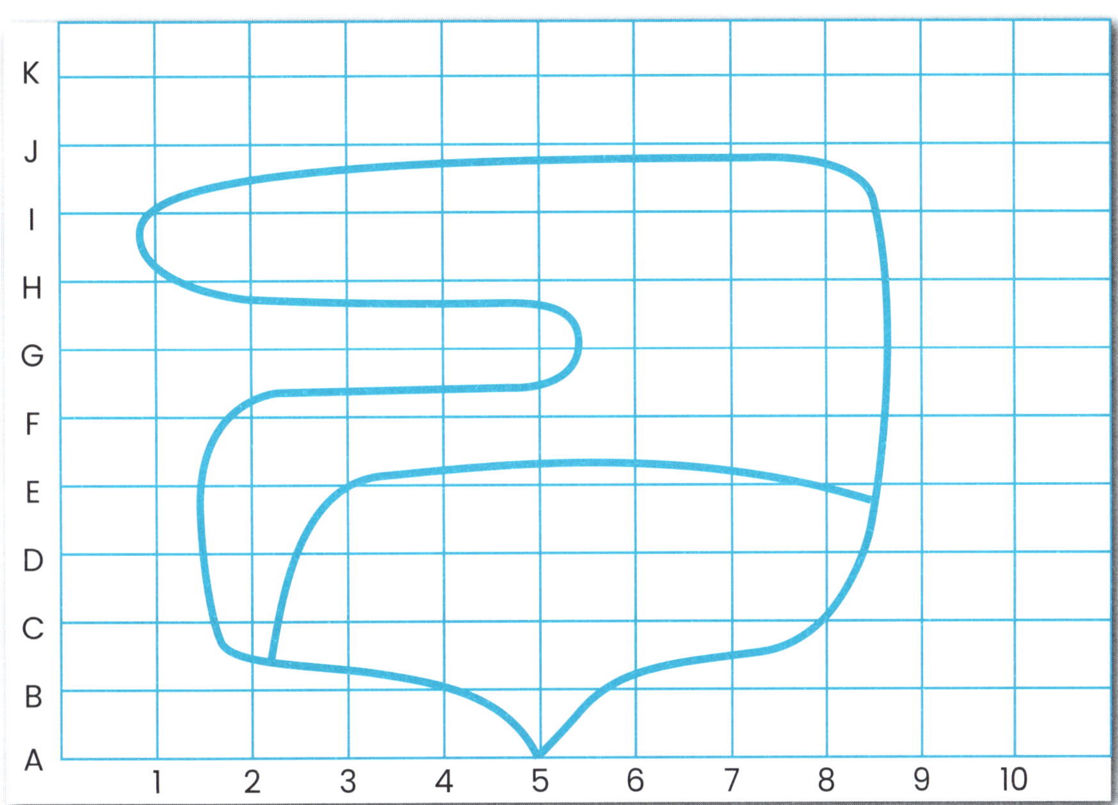

10 Here is the key for the map. Copy the icons onto the correct locations on the map.

E Entry/Exit at 5A

S zoo shop at 5B

giraffes at 8C

ice creams at 5D

elephants at 5J

kangaroos at 1E

chimpanzees at 6G

reptiles at 9G

aquarium at 2B

public toilets at 4B, 2F, 8I, 3H

11 Shade the picnic area from 3C to 7C to 7F to 3F to 3C.

12 If you wanted to buy a gift, where would you go on the map? ______

NUMBER AND ALGEBRA

1 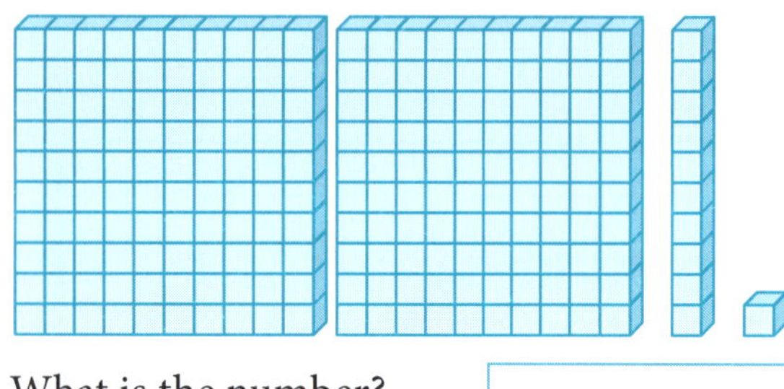

What is the number?

2 43, 34, 33

Write the numbers in sequence from smallest to largest.

3 Which number is closest to 26?

A 21 B twelve
C thirty D 62

4 What is the value of the hundreds digit in 321?

5 Write the next three numbers in the pattern.

12, 14, 16, 18, ___, ___, ___

6 Draw the next three shapes in the pattern.

7 Double 10 is

8 Complete the table.

+	100	200	300	400
350				

9 17 + 14 has the same value as

20 + ___

10
$$\begin{array}{r} 85 \\ -\ 15 \\ \hline \end{array}$$

11 Draw an arrow on the number line to show starting at 72 and going backwards 9.

60 61 62 63 64 65 66 67 68 69 70 71 72 73 74 75

Write a number sentence to match.

12 Tiffany had 30 marbles. She lost 11 but bought 8 more. How many does she have now?

13 Draw three groups of six children. How many children are there?

14 The roller-coaster has five carriages. Each carriage holds five people. Which one helps work out how many people can fit on the roller-coaster?

A 5 + 5 B 5 × 5
C 25 – 5 D 5 × 2

NUMBER AND ALGEBRA

1 Divide 27 by 3 using arrows to jump along the number line.

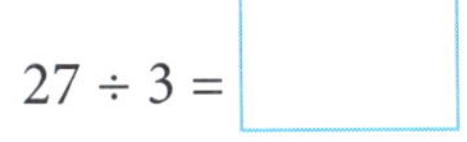

0 1 2 3 4 5 6 7 8 9 10 11 12 13 14 15 16 17 18 19 20 21 22 23 24 25 26 27

27 ÷ 3 =

2 18 children need to share 6 books. How many children will share each book?

3  

If the shapes are folded along the dotted lines, which shape(s) will fold into two equal halves?

A  B  C  D 

4 Circle two price tags that add up to $4.50.

5 Circle the coins Charlotte will use to pay for groceries that cost six dollars and ten cents.

MEASUREMENT AND SPACE

6 05:30 Write the time in words.

7 Draw hands on the clock to show half past seven.

8 If 3 May is a Friday, what day of the week is 6 May?

9 Colour an area that is equal to 6 squares.

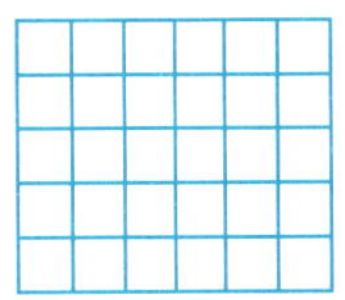

10 Describe this shape.

11 Which object has the shape of a cylinder?

A  B  C  D 

12 Circle the star that is in between the two shaded stars.

13 Here is an arrow. 

Draw the arrow after a quarter turn anticlockwise.

STATISTICS AND PROBABILITY

14 There are ten milk chocolates and two dark chocolates in a barrel.

Dad likes dark chocolate. What are his chances of getting a dark chocolate if he selects one without looking?

A certain
B likely
C unlikely
D impossible

NUMBER AND ALGEBRA

1

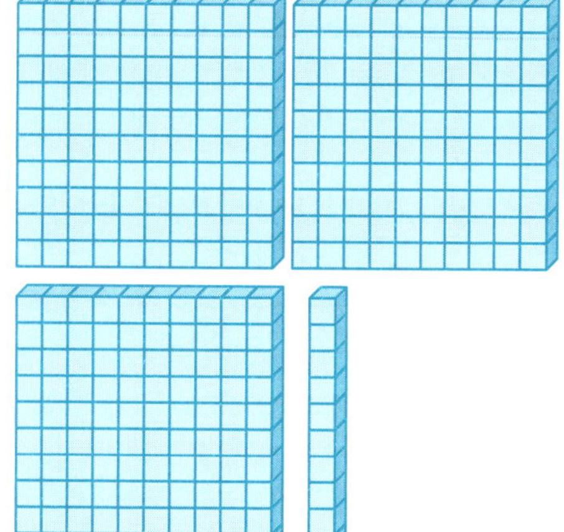

What is the number?

2 55, 15, 51

Write the numbers in sequence from smallest to largest.

3 Which number is closest to 39?

A 29 B 92 C twenty-five D 48

4 Write 751 in words.

5 Write the next three numbers in the pattern.

17, 24, 31, ☐, ☐, ☐

6 Draw the shape that comes next in the pattern.

Ξ Ξ O ΞΞ Π Ξ Ξ O ΞΞ

7 16 + 4 has the same value as

15 + ☐

8 Complete the table.

+	100	200	300	400
50				

9 13 + 16 has the same value as

20 + ☐

10

$$\begin{array}{r} 85 \\ -\ 25 \\ \hline \end{array} \qquad \begin{array}{r} 95 \\ -\ 25 \\ \hline \end{array}$$

11 Show your working on the number line.

35 36 37 38 39 40 41 42 43 44 45 46 47 48 49 50

46 – 8 = ☐

12 Harald had 25 coloured pencils. He gave 5 to his sister. How many did he have left?

13 Draw two groups of eight children. How many children are there?

14 The class worked in six groups of four for maths. Which one helps you work out how many children were in the class?

A 4 + 4 + 4 + 4 B 6 + 6 + 6 + 6
C 4 + 6 D 6 × 4

NUMBER AND ALGEBRA

1 Divide 28 into groups of 7 using the number line.

0 1 2 3 4 5 6 7 8 9 10 11 12 13 14 15 16 17 18 19 20 21 22 23 24 25 26 27 28

How many groups of 7 are there?

2 There are 6 scissors for 12 children. How many children need to share each pair of scissors?

3

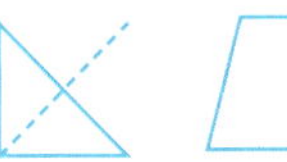
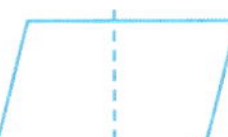
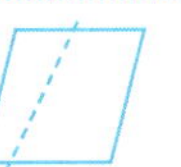
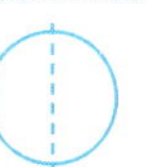

If the shapes are folded along the dotted lines, which shapes will fold into two equal halves?

A

B

C

D

4 Circle two price tags that add up to $4.00.

5 How much money will be left if Theon buys noodles that cost six dollars and seventy-five cents?

MEASUREMENT AND SPACE

6 08:30 Write the time in words.

7 Write the time in words.

8 If 29 October is a Wednesday, what date is the following Friday?

9 Colour an area that is equal to 8 squares.

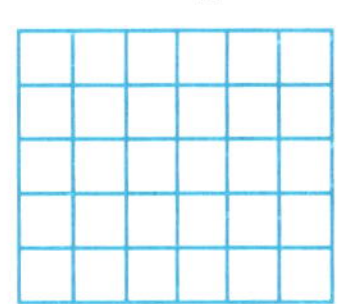

10 Colour the shapes that have 4 straight sides.

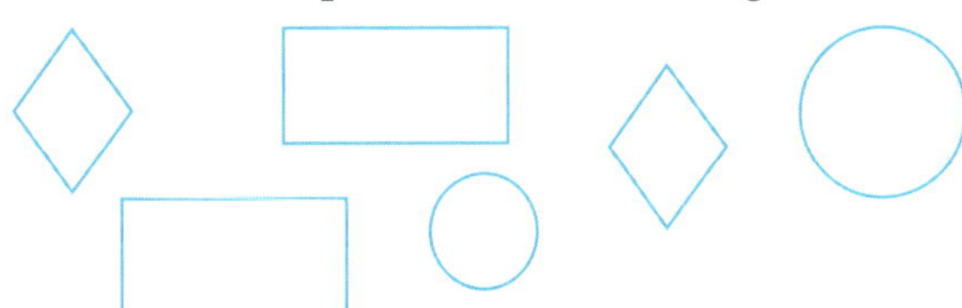

11 Which shape is **not** suitable for stacking on a shop shelf?

A
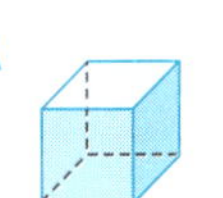

B

C

D

12 Circle the star that is to the far right of the shaded star.

13 Draw the shape a half turn to the right.

L

STATISTICS AND PROBABILITY

14 There are 10 red frogs and 10 green frogs in a pack of 20 frogs.

What are the chances of getting a black frog?

A certain **B** likely

C unlikely **D** impossible

A day in the life of a dragon

Show your working out in number sentences or drawings.

NUMBER AND ALGEBRA

1. The dragons ate 4 sheep on Monday, 2 on Tuesday, 3 on Wednesday and then 2 every day for the rest of the week. How many sheep did they eat?

2. Daisy the dragon slept for 5 hours before she went hunting and another 3 hours after breakfast. How many hours did she sleep altogether?

3. Once upon a time, there were 25 dragons in the mountains but now there are only 2. How many dragons have disappeared?

4. There are 100 people living in the village at the foot of the mountain. Forty of them are children. How many adults are there?

5. If a dragon can walk 8 km in one hour, how far will it walk in half an hour?

MEASUREMENT AND SPACE

6. Daisy arrived back at her cave at seven o'clock. She'd been hunting for 2 hours. What time did she go out?

7. She flew from her cave to Black Mountain and back. It is a distance of 3 kilometres. How far did she fly?

8. When Daisy flew north, the village was on her left. When she flew south, which side was the village on?

   A north **B** south
   C left **D** right

STATISTICS AND PROBABILITY

9. Dragons live in fairytales. Are you likely to see one flying over your home?

   A maybe
   B yes
   C one chance in three
   D no

MEASUREMENT AND SPACE

10 Read the text below. Use lines and arrows to mark Poppy's journey on the map.

Poppy saw a dragon in the sky. She wanted to know where the dragon lived. She ran out the back door of her house. Then she ran straight across the backyard, jumped over the back fence and ran into the forest. She worked her way around a number of big trees. She could still see the dragon above the forest. She reached the stream. She turned right and followed the stream east until she arrived at a fallen log that reached across the stream to the other side. She walked across the log.

11 Answer the questions about Poppy's journey.

a In which direction was the forest from the house?

A north **B** south **C** east **D** west

b In which direction did she walk across the log?

A north **B** south **C** east **D** west

c In which direction is the playground from Poppy's house?

A north **B** south **C** east **D** west

d The stream runs

A north–south. **B** east–west. **C** sideways. **D** backwards.

e In which direction is Poppy's house from the forest?

A north **B** south **C** east **D** west

12 Draw a cow across the road and south-west of Poppy's house.

NUMBER AND ALGEBRA

1 Expand the numbers.

65 = ☐ hundreds ☐ tens ☐ ones

142 = ☐ hundreds ☐ tens ☐ ones

2 56, 65, 16

Write the numbers in sequence from smallest to largest.

☐

3 Which number is closest to 19? ☐

A sixty-nine B 49
C twenty-nine D eighteen

4 Write 924 in words.

☐

5 Write the next three numbers in the pattern.

65, 62, 59, 56, ☐, ☐, ☐

6 Draw the two shapes that come next in the pattern.

ΘΔΘΘΔΘΘΔΘ

7 13 + 7 has the same value as

12 + ☐

8 Complete the table.

+	150	250	350	450
50				

9 11 + 99 has the same value as

10 + ☐

10

$$\begin{array}{r} 88 \\ -\ 17 \\ \hline \end{array} \qquad \begin{array}{r} 98 \\ -\ 17 \\ \hline \end{array}$$

11 Show your working on the number line. Start at 71 and jump back 9. Write a number sentence to match the number line.

58 59 60 61 62 63 64 65 66 67 68 69 70 71 72 73 74 75

Where do you land? ☐

12 Willow had 25 toffees. She gave 20 to friends. How many toffees did she have left? ☐

13 Draw three groups of eight marbles. How many marbles are there? ☐

14 Eighteen children used their handprints to paint a mural. Which one helps you work out how many handprints were on the mural? ☐

A 18 ÷ 2 B 18 + 2
C 6 + 6 + 6 D 18 × 2

NUMBER AND ALGEBRA

1 Divide 18 by 6 using arrows to jump along the number line.

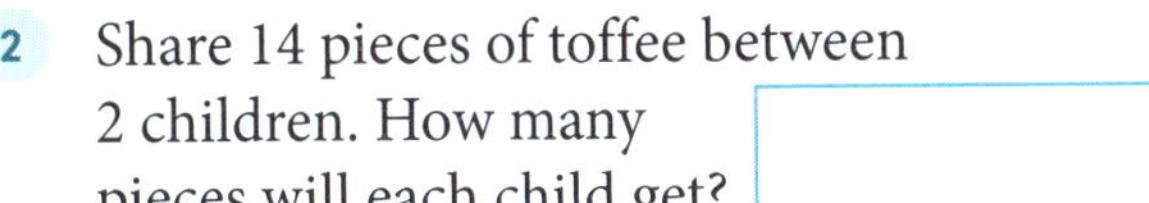

How many groups of 6 are there?

2 Share 14 pieces of toffee between 2 children. How many pieces will each child get?

3 Draw dotted lines to divide each object in half.

4 I have six dollars and fifty cents. Write the amount in numbers.

5 Leiling has

How much money will be left if Leiling buys a bag of peanuts that costs two dollars and forty cents?

MEASUREMENT AND SPACE

6 11:30 Write the time in words.

7 Draw hands on the clock to show half past ten.

8 If 30 July is a Saturday, what date is the following Monday?

9 What is the perimeter of the shaded rectangle?

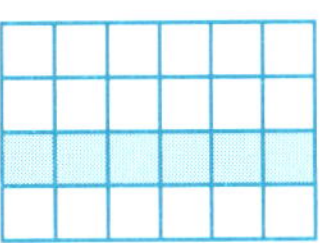

10 Describe this shape.

11 Which one is the shape of a rectangular prism?

A 

B 

C 

D 

12 Circle the flower that is below and to the left of the shaded flower

13 Flip the triangle over the line and draw it.

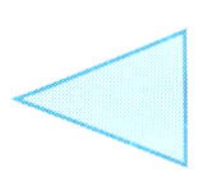

STATISTICS AND PROBABILITY

14 There are twenty red frogs in a pack of red frogs.

What is the likelihood of getting a red frog?

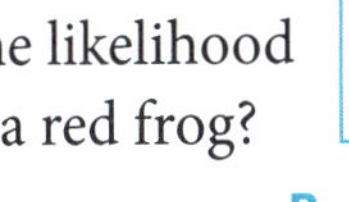

A certain B likely
C unlikely D impossible

NUMBER AND ALGEBRA

1

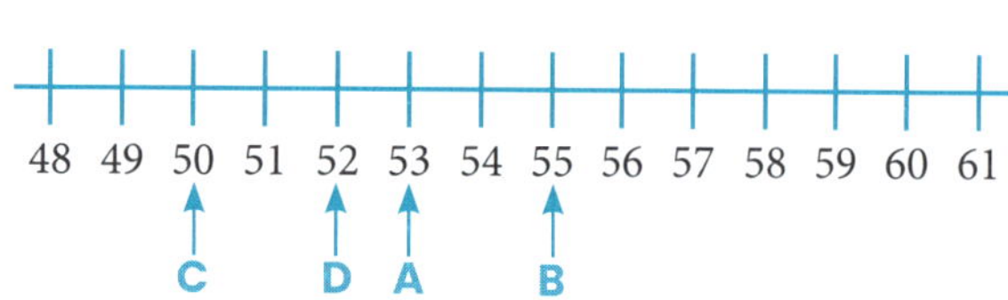

Which arrow points to the number 53 on the number line?

2 28, 18, 81, 82

Write the numbers in sequence from smallest to largest.

3 Which number is closest to 51?

A 15
B fifty
C 54
D forty

4 Write 543 in words.

5 The rule for this pattern is double each number and add 1. Write the next two numbers.

2, 5, 11, ___, ___

6 Draw the next two cards in the pattern.

7 39 + 11 has the same value as

40 + ___

8 Complete the table.

+	250	350	450	550
50				

9 21 + 29 has the same value as

___ + 30

10

11 Show your working on the number line.

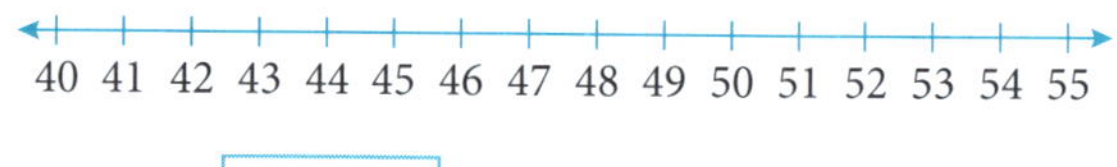

52 – 8 = ___

12 Mei had 20 apples for 14 horses. Thirteen horses ate one apple each. One horse ate two. How many apples were left over?

13 Draw 6 groups of 4 marbles. How many marbles are there?

14 Five groups of students need two sheets of cardboard for each group. Which one helps work out how many are needed altogether?

A 5 + 5 + 5 + 5
B 10 ÷ 5
C 5 × 2
D 12 + 2

NUMBER AND ALGEBRA

1 Divide 18 into groups of 6 using the number line.

0 1 2 3 4 5 6 7 8 9 10 11 12 13 14 15 16 17 18 19

Write a number sentence to match.

2 Garry and Phillip share 22 strawberries equally. How many will Garry get?

3 Draw dotted lines to divide each object in half.

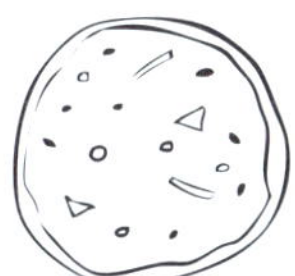
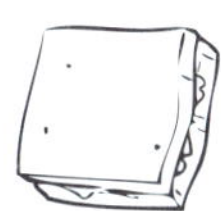

4 I have eight dollars and fifteen cents. Write the amount in numbers.

5 How much money will be left if Isabella buys two health bars that cost $1.50 each?

MEASUREMENT AND SPACE

6 7:30 Write the time in words.

7 Draw hands on the clock to show half past two.

8 If 30 July is a Saturday, what date is the Thursday before?

9 What is the area of the shaded rectangle? Remember that the area is all of the surface of the shape. Measure it in squares.

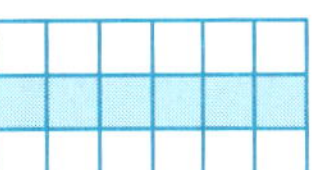

10 Colour the shapes that have four corners.

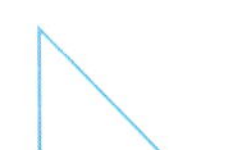
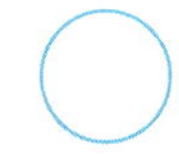

11 Which one has the shape of a sphere?

A

B

C

D
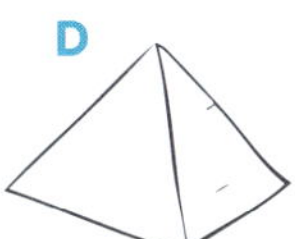

12 James chose the cupcake that was second from the left in the top row. Circle the one he chose.

13 Draw the arrow after it has made a full turn clockwise.

STATISTICS AND PROBABILITY

14 There are 12 red frogs and 4 green frogs in a pack of frogs.

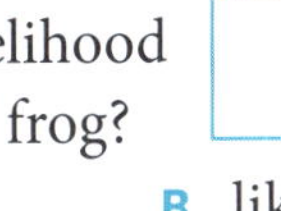

What is the likelihood of getting a red frog?

A certain **B** likely

C unlikely **D** impossible

Nature and the seasons

Show your working out in number sentences or drawings.

NUMBER AND ALGEBRA

1 One bee visited 90 flowers to collect pollen. Another bee visited 80 flowers. Which one helps you work out how many flowers were visited altogether?

A 90 + 80 B 170 – 90
C 120 + 90 D 90 – 80

2 Josephine walks 5 kilometres every weekday and 10 kilometres on Saturdays. Which ones help work out how far she walks each week?

A 5 + 5 + 5 + 5 + 5 + 5 + 10
B 5 + 5 + 5 + 5 + 5 +10
C 5 + 5 + 5 + 5 + 5 + 5 + 5
D 5 × 5 + 10

3 Sixty chickens are in the paddock. Twelve are sunbaking. The rest are pecking for food. Which one helps you work out how many are pecking for food?

A 60 ÷ 12 B 60 + 12
C 60 – 12 D 12 + 48

4 The class planted 150 trees. Twenty-five were red river gums. The rest were black box. Which one helps work out the number of black box planted?

A 150 + 25 B 150 ÷ 25
C 150 – 25 D 25 × ___ = 150

5 Eddie bought 25 grevilleas. He planted 16 on Saturday and the rest on Sunday. Which one helps work out how many he planted on Sunday?

A 16 – 25 B 25 × 16
C 25 + 16 D 25 – 16

MEASUREMENT AND SPACE

6 Izzy went for a one-and-a-quarter hour walk. She left home at ten o'clock. What time did she get back?

A 10:15 B 10:30 C 11:15 D 11:30

7 Which season follows summer?

8 Winter ends on 30 August. Which months are in spring?

STATISTICS AND PROBABILITY

9 Read the temperature and suggest which season it's most likely to be.

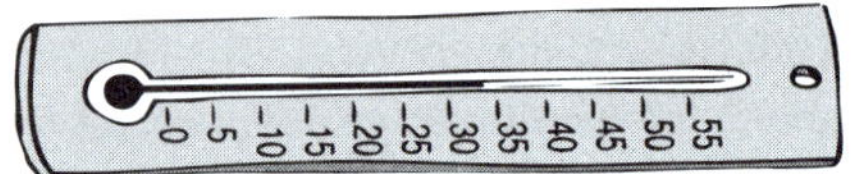

MEASUREMENT AND SPACE

Maria's weather record

FEBRUARY 2020						
Monday	Tuesday	Wednesday	Thursday	Friday	Saturday	Sunday
					1	2
3	4	5	6	7	8	9
10	11	12	13	14	15	16
17	18	19	20	21	22	23
24	25	26	27	28	29	

	Extra hot
	Sunny
	Wet

10 a How many days were extra hot? ______

b How many days were sunny? ______

c How many days were wet? ______

d How many more sunny days were there than wet days? ______

e What type of weather was it for most of February 2020? ______

f How many days were there in this month? ______

g How many days are there usually in February? ______

h Why does February on the calendar have 29 days? ______

i February is in which season? ______

11 Draw the data from the calendar in the graph.

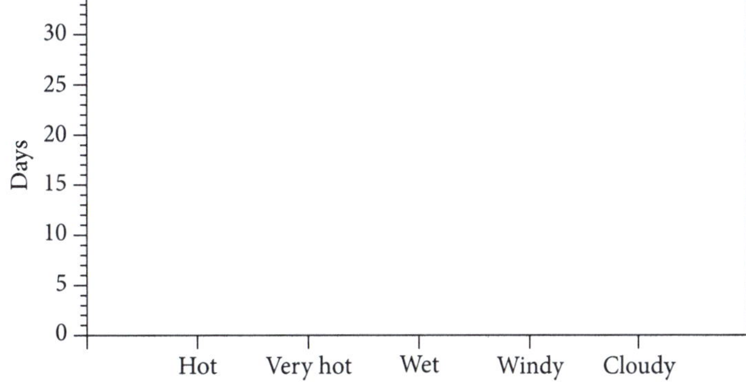

12 Does the graph make it easier or harder to compare information about the weather? Why?

______

NUMBER AND ALGEBRA

1 Write the number that has 5 tens, 0 ones and 4 hundreds.

2 Which number is largest?

A 787 B 789
C 899 D 988

3 Which number is closest to 91?

A 61 B 40
C 30 D 19

4 Write 230 in words.

5 Write the next three numbers in the pattern.

1, 6, 11, 16, ☐, ☐, ☐

6 ✪◆✪★★★✪◆✪★★★✪◆✪

In the pattern, how many ✪ are needed for each ◆?

7

18 + 2 has the same value as

14 + ☐

8 Complete the table.

+	25	50	75	100
800				

9

18 + 15 has the same value as

28 + ☐

10

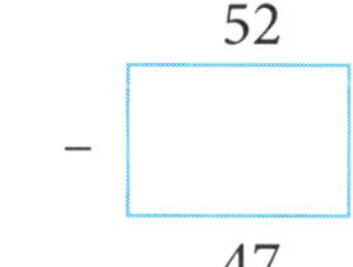

$52 - \square = 47$

$52 - 47 = \square$

11 Show your working on the number line.

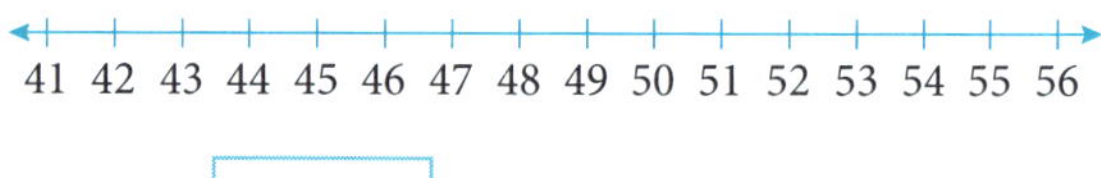

53 – 9 = ☐

12 Mum bought a box of 100 nails.
She used 16.
How many were left?

13 Draw three groups of four stars.

14 Dad bought two cartons of eggs. Each carton holds twelve eggs. How many eggs does he have?

NUMBER AND ALGEBRA

1 Divide 100 into groups of 10. How many groups are there?

2 Share 30 sweets between 5 children. How many will each child get?

3 Draw dotted lines to divide each object into two equal halves.

4   

What is the total value of the three coins?

5 Circle the exact coins Luisa needs to buy two apples that cost 80c each.

MEASUREMENT AND SPACE

6 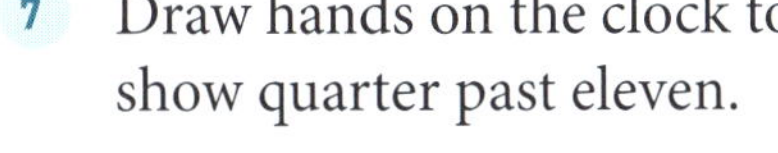

Write the time in words.

7 Draw hands on the clock to show quarter past eleven.

8 March, April and May are autumn months. In which month does winter start?

9 How many squares is the shaded area?

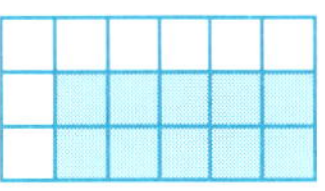

10 How is a square the same as a rectangle?

11 Which one is a cube?

A 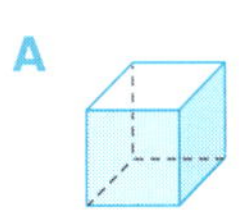 B C 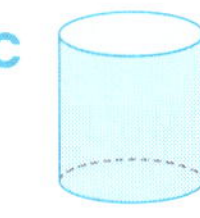

C E 

12 Draw a cross in the square that is two squares to the right of the existing cross.

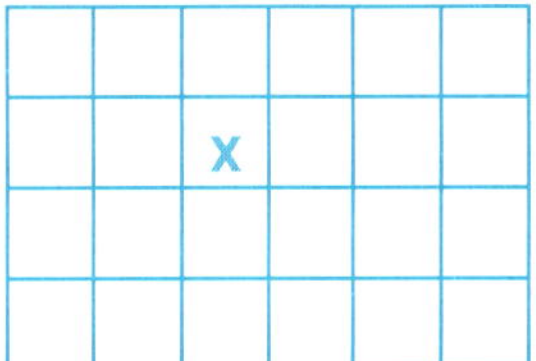

13 Which puzzle piece matches the space?

A  B  C  D 

STATISTICS AND PROBABILITY

14 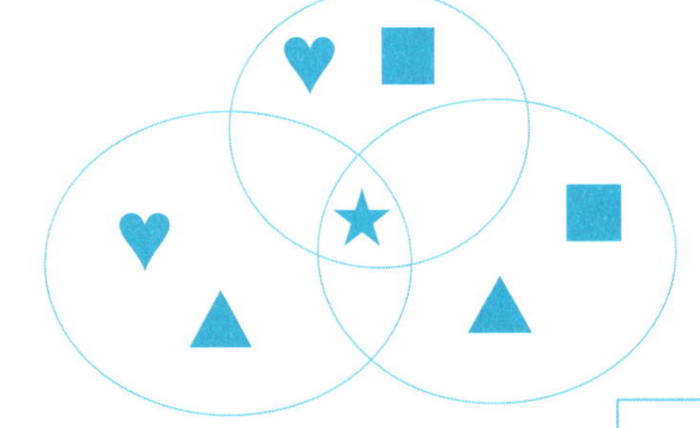

Which shape is in all three circles?

A heart B triangle C star D square

NUMBER AND ALGEBRA

1 Write the number in words that has 0 tens, 4 ones and 9 hundreds.

2 Which number is smallest?

A 1200 B 112
C 429 D 42

3 Which number is closest to 14?

A 31 B 12
C 19 D 52

4 Write 209 in words.

5 Write the next two numbers in the pattern.

1, 7, 13, 19, ☐, ☐

6 ✚✚●✚✚✚●✚✚✚●✚✚✚●✚✚✚●✚✚✚●✚

In the pattern, how many ✚ are needed for each ●?

7

12 + ☐ = 20

12 + ☐ = 30

8 Complete the table.

+	10	20	30	40
900				

9

17 + 23 has the same value as

20 + ☐

10

62 – ☐ = 57

62 – 57 = ☐

11 Show your working on the number line.

72 73 74 75 76 77 78 79 80 81 82 83 84 85 86 87 88 89 90 91 92

92 – 16 = ☐

12 Sharna had 

She spent 30c. How much money was left?

13 Draw four groups of three stars.

14 The canteen bought three cartons of eggs. Each carton holds a dozen eggs. How many eggs are there?

NUMBER AND ALGEBRA

1 Share 50 paper clips between 10 children. How many paper clips will each one get?

2 Share 20 pencils between 3 children.

a How many pencils will each child get?

b How many pencils will be left over?

3 Draw a shape that can be divided into two equal halves.

4

What is the total value of the coins?

5 Circle the coins Lina should use to buy a banana that costs 50c and an apple that costs 60c.

MEASUREMENT AND SPACE

6 09:15 Write the time in words.

7 Draw hands on the clock to show 09:00.

8 Which season follows spring?

9 What is the area of the shaded rectangle?

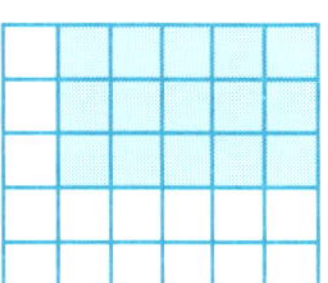

10 What do these shapes have in common?

11 How many faces does a cube have?

12 Draw a cross in each square that is two squares away from the cross.

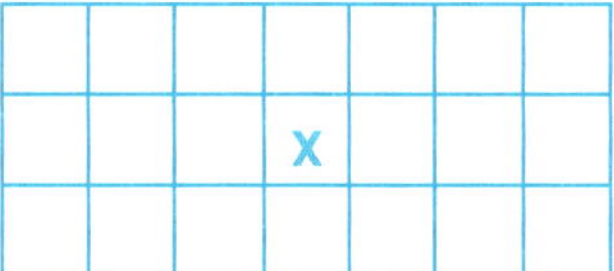

13 Which puzzle piece matches the space?

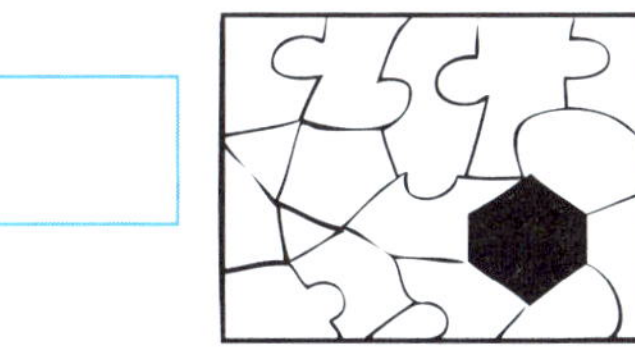

A  B  C 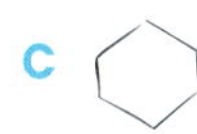 D 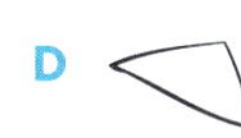

STATISTICS AND PROBABILITY

14

D H C E A B F G

Which letter is in all the circles?

Fun and games

Show your working out in number sentences or drawings.

NUMBER AND ALGEBRA

1 Max and Zara have 12 pieces left to finish from their jigsaw. It has 100 pieces. How many pieces have they completed?

A 100 + 12 B 100 × 12
C 82 + 12 D 100 – 12

2 Five groups of four children is the same number of children as four groups of

A 3 B 10
C 4 D 5

3 Twenty-five children need to make even teams for a game. How many teams can there be? Which number sentence helps to answer the question?

A 4 teams of 5
B 6 teams of 5
C 5 teams of 5
D 4 teams of 4

4 A class of 30 children needs to divide into even groups for a game. There can be no more than 7 children in each group. How many groups could there be? Choose all the possible answers.

A 7 B 5 C 6 D 4

5 Lotte had 17 chocolates which she and four friends shared fairly.

a How many chocolates did they each get?
b How many chocolates were left over?

MEASUREMENT AND SPACE

6 Jodie ran the 100-m race in 41 seconds. Tamara was faster by 4 seconds. How long did Tamara take?

7 Farid is good at long jump. The length of his jump would be measured as

A 4.1 km. B 4.1 metres.
C 4.1 centimetres. D 4.1 degrees.

8 Do some research. Which of these sports have sphere-shaped balls?

A cricket B tennis C softball/baseball
D AFL E rugby league
F squash G volleyball H table tennis
I bowling J netball/basketball
K hockey L soccer

STATISTICS AND PROBABILITY

9 If Marty's team practises really hard for the next month, their chances of winning some matches are

A more likely. B the same.
C certain. D less likely.

MEASUREMENT AND SPACE

10 Kabil and Avra made a robot.

Circle yes or no if you think Kabil and Avra used these shapes to construct their robot.

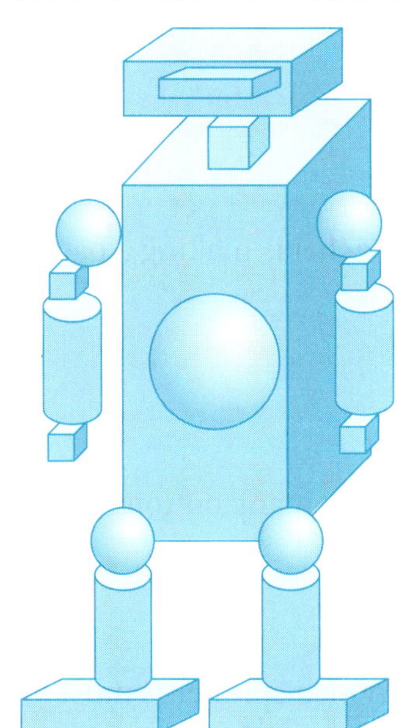

a sphere yes no

b triangular prism yes no

c rectangular prism yes no

d cube yes no

e pyramid yes no

f cylinder yes no

11 Draw lines to link the labels to the objects.

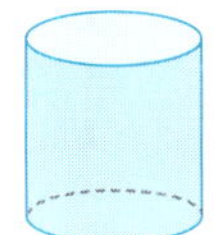 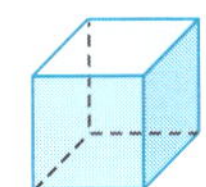 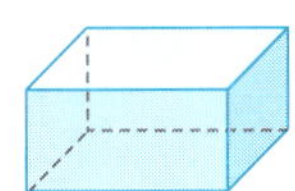  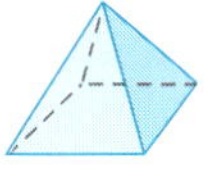 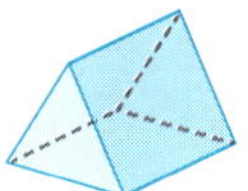

sphere | triangular prism | rectangular prism | cube | pyramid | cylinder

12 Design a robot of your own that uses 3D shapes.

NAPLAN-STYLE TEST 1

1 Which of these pictures shows a cylinder?

A

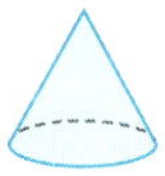

B

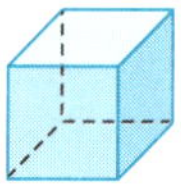

C

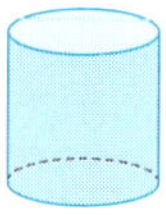

D

2 Rachel is making a pattern.

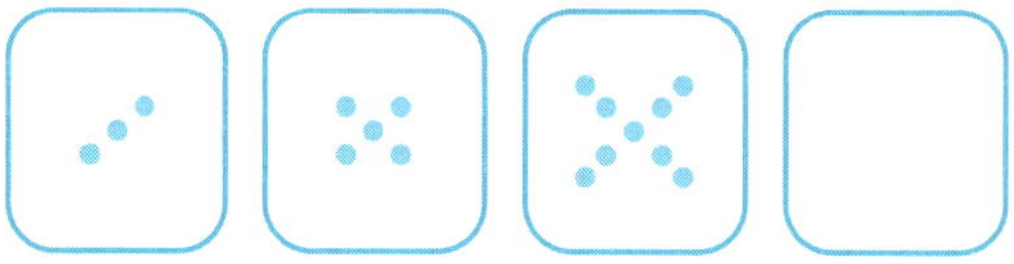

How many buttons will be in the next box?

A 10

B 14

C 15

D 13

3 Which spinner is most likely to stop on white?

A

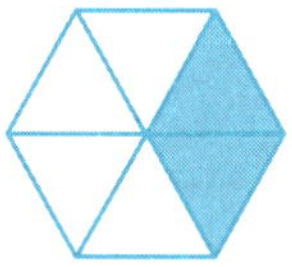

B

C

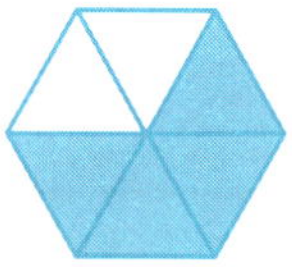

D

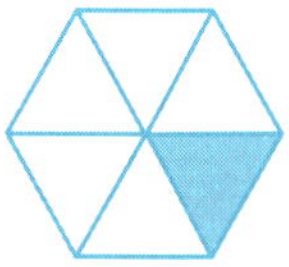

4 Mark has these coins.

How much money does he have?

A $4.10

B $4.00

C $4.25

D $3.90

5 Johanna drew a picture of her fish tank.

Which fish is second from the bottom of the tank?

A 

B 

C 

D 

6 Four groups of five children is the same number of children as five groups of

A 3
B 10
C 4
D 5

7 97 – 77 = ?

A 27
B 17
C 20
D 70

8 Which rectangle is a quarter turn to the right?

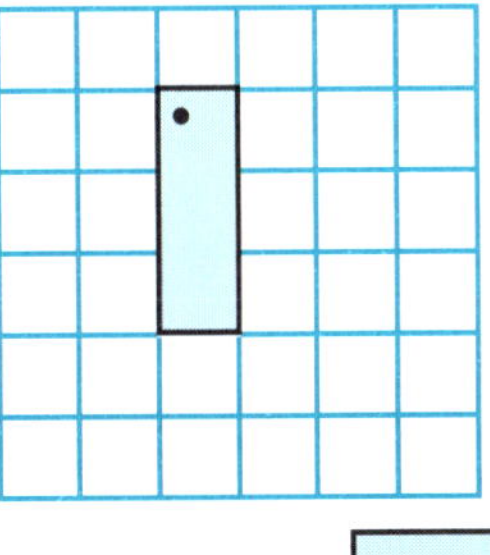

A

B

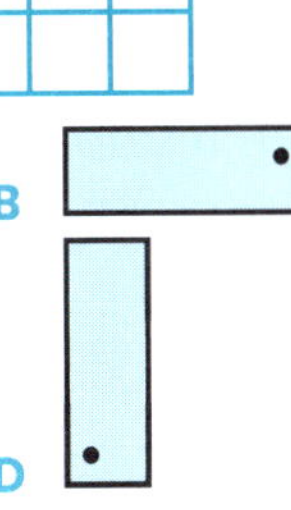

C

D

9 Which shape is in all the circles?

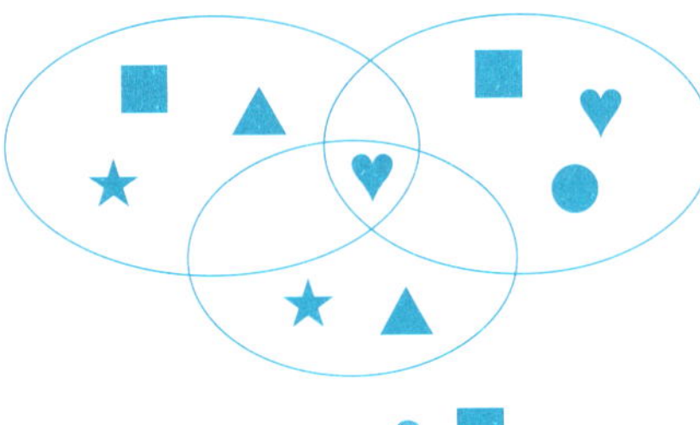

A ♥
B ●
C ■
D ▲

10 How many friends can share the chocolate equally?

Choose all the correct answers.

A 2
B 5
C 4
D 10

11 Which number is missing?

5, 10, 15, ____, 25

A 15
B 30
C 16
D 20

12 The bucket holds 12 litres when full.

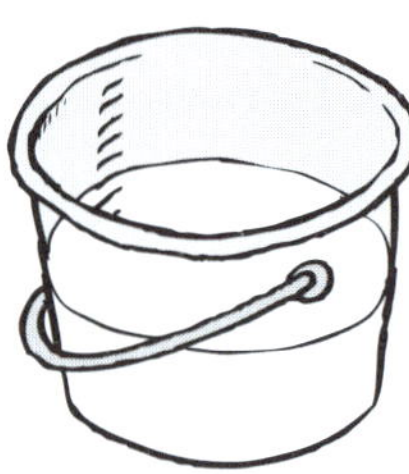

How much water is in the bucket?

A 6 litres
B 8 litres
C 10 litres
D 12 litres

13 There were 15 people in the queue. Six more people joined the queue.

One person left the queue. Which number sentence will help work out how many people are now in the queue?

A 15 – 6 – 1
B 15 × 6
C 15 + 6 + 1
D 15 + 6 – 1

14 Fifty people were in the cinema. Forty were eating snacks.

Which number sentence will help work out how many people were **not** eating snacks?

A 50 + 40
B 50 – 40
C 40 + 50 = 90
D 50 ÷ 40

15 Start at 32 and count back 3.

A 31
B 28
C 35
D 29

16 Minh and Fee have 42 stickers altogether. Minh has 24.

Which one helps to find the number of stickers Fee has?

A 42 – 24
B 66 – 42
C 42 + 24
D 42 + 18

17 The graph shows the favourite fruit of children in Ms Draper's Year 2 class. Which statement is true?

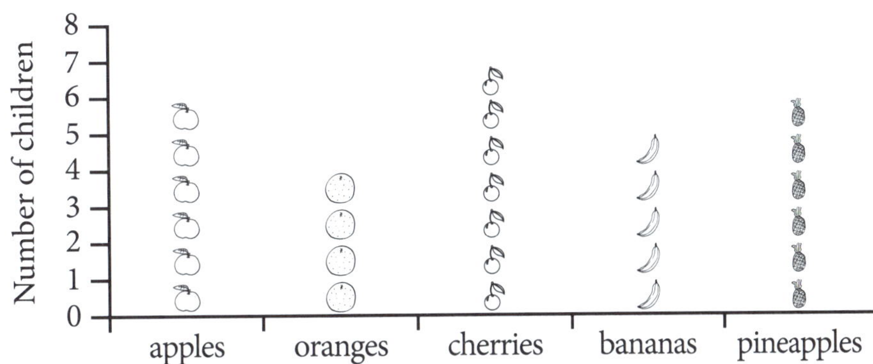

A More children like pineapples than apples.
B Pineapple is the most popular fruit.
C Bananas are the least popular fruit.
D Cherries are the most popular fruit.

18 Which clock shows quarter past three?

A 
B
C 
D

19 Raksha rode her bike to school. Which was the first building Raksha passed on her right?

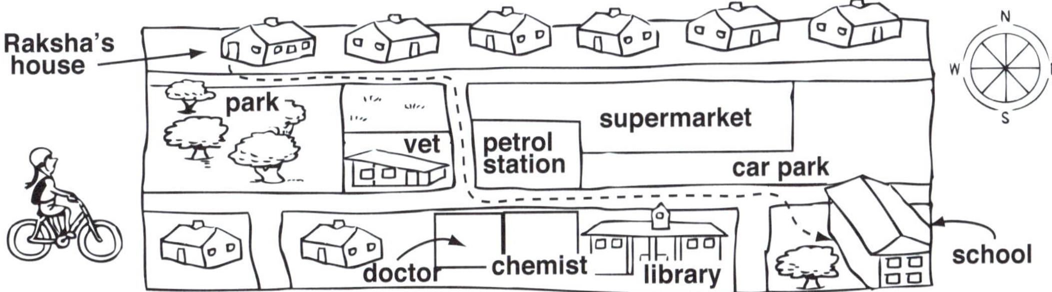

A petrol station
B supermarket
C doctor
D vet

20 Kyle's birthday is 30 April. His friend's birthday is five days after his.

APRIL						
Monday	Tuesday	Wednesday	Thursday	Friday	Saturday	Sunday
	1	2	3	4	5	6
7	8	9	10	11	12	13
14	15	16	17	18	19	20
21	22	23	24	25	26	27
28	29	30				

What day of the week will that be?

A Sunday
B Monday
C Tuesday
D Wednesday

NUMBER AND ALGEBRA

1 Write the number that has 8 tens, 9 ones and 0 hundreds.

2 Which number is largest?

A 111
B 121
C 112
D 110

3 Which number is closest to 65?

A 56 B 60
C 71 D 59

4 Write 981 in words.

5 Write the next three numbers in the pattern.

22, 19, 16, ___, ___, ___

6 ■■■★■■■★■■■

In the pattern, how many ■ are needed for each ★?

7 Write a number sentence to match the number line.

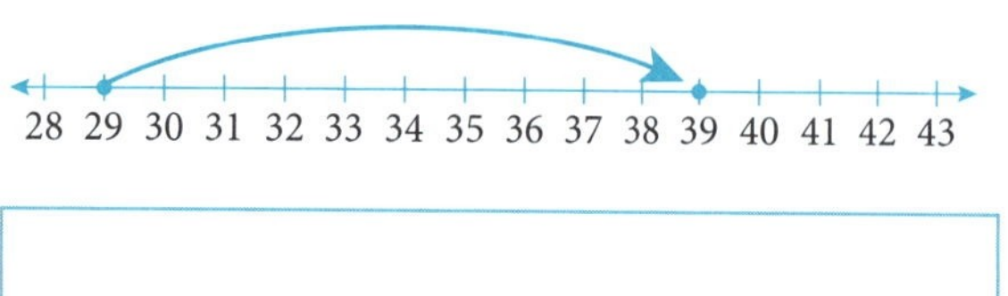

8 Complete the table.

+	100	200	300	400
150				

9 39 + 11 has the same value as

40 + ___

10

47 − ___ = 27

47 − 27 = ___

11 Nonno cooked a dozen scones and ate 3. How many were left?

12 Robbie had

He spent 40c. How much money did he have left?

13 Lily has twice as many pencils as Steven. Steven has ten. How many does Lily have?

14 The canteen bought four cartons of baked beans. Each carton holds 12 cans. Which one helps work out the total number of cans?

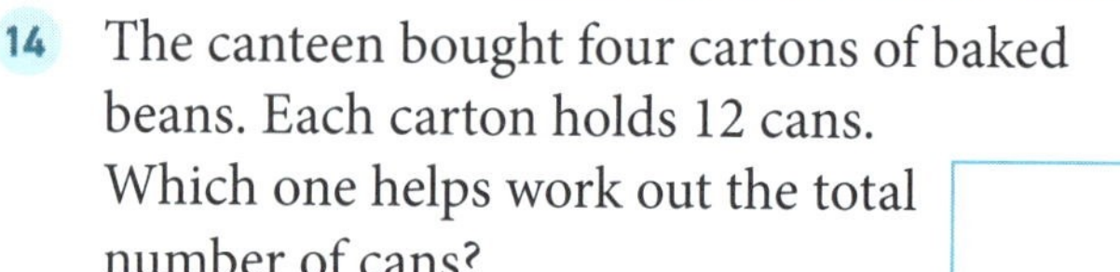

A 12 + 12 + 12
B 12 × 12
C 3 × 12
D 4 × 12

NUMBER AND ALGEBRA

1 Divide 40 notepads into stacks of 10. How many stacks are there?

2 Ten children want to paint five murals for the library. How many children will paint each mural?

3 Divide the cake into equal halves.

4

What is the total value of the coins?

5 Circle the coins that Scarlet should use to buy two bananas that cost 50c each.

MEASUREMENT AND SPACE

6 Write the time in words.

7 Draw hands on the clock to show quarter past ten.

8 The scale is balanced. What is the weight of the ?

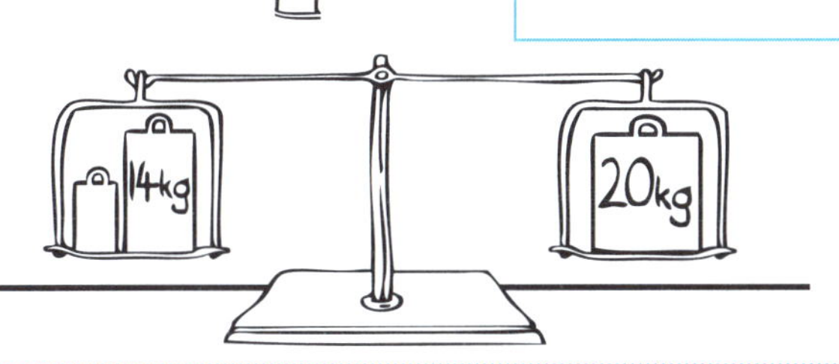

9 Which season comes before spring?

10 A triangle has

sides and corners.

11 I am a can of soup. What shape am I?

A cone B cube
C sphere D cylinder

12 What shape is at A3?

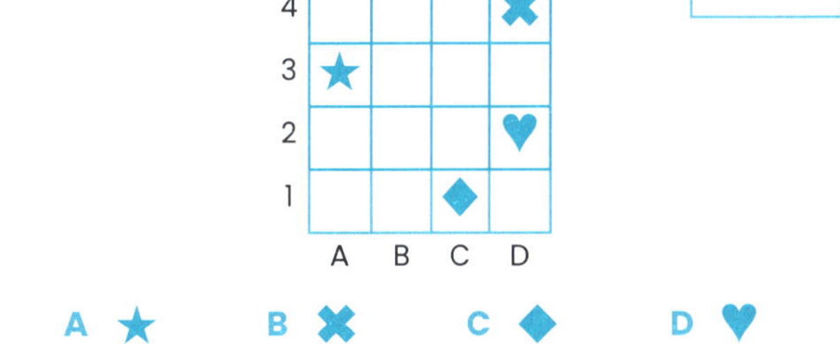

A ★ B ✖ C ◆ D ♥

13 Flip the rectangle across the line.

STATISTICS AND PROBABILITY

14 Add up the tally marks.

Books borrowed in Term 1	Tally	Total
Tilly	𝍸 𝍸 𝍸 ||	
Brandon	𝍸 𝍸 𝍸 ||||	
George	𝍸 𝍸 𝍸 𝍸 𝍸	

NUMBER AND ALGEBRA

1 Write the number that has 9 ones, 2 tens and 3 hundreds.

2 Which number is largest?

A 987 **B** 988

C 909 **D** 997

3 Which number is closest to 14?

A 139

B 142

C 114

D 144

4 Write 440 in words.

5 Write the next three numbers in the pattern

20, 25, 30, 35, ___, ___, ___

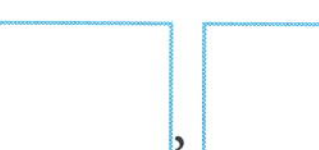

6 ⊙⊙⊙■⊙⊙⊙■⊙⊙⊙■⊙ …

In the pattern, how many ■ are needed for three ⊙?

7 Write a number sentence to match the number line.

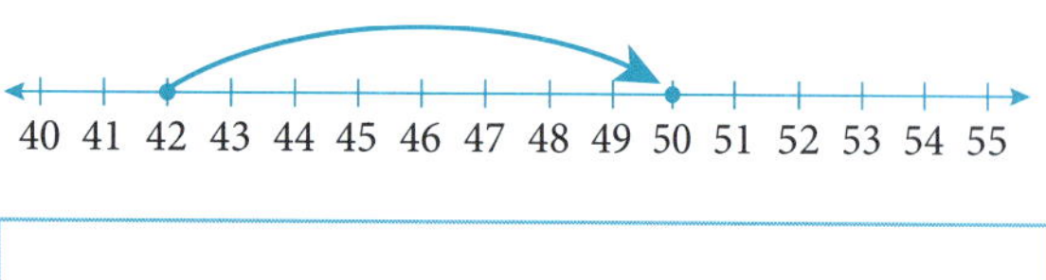

8 Complete the table.

+	50	150	250	350
250				

9 25 + 26 has the same value as

50 + ___

10 56 – ___ = 48

56 – 48 = ___

11 Edith had 12 cherries. She ate four. How many were left?

12 Jeremy had $1. He spent 75c. How much money did he have left?

13 4 + 4 + 4 + 4 + 4 is the same as

___ × 4

14 Dad bought two packets of pegs. Each pack had 24 pegs. Which two answers help you work out how many pegs Dad got altogether?

A 2 × 24 **B** 24 ÷ 2

C 24 + 2 **D** 24 + 24

NUMBER AND ALGEBRA

1 Divide 40 notepads into stacks of 5. How many stacks are there?

2 Raksha brought twelve pineapple slices to school to share with her friends Inga and Minh. How many slices will each child get?

3 Sophie bought six oranges for the soccer team. Each child will get half an orange. How many children are on the team?

4

What is the total value of the coins?

5 How much change will Lucy get if she buys two bananas that cost 50c each?

MEASUREMENT AND SPACE

6 12:15 Write the time in words.

7 Draw hands on the clock to show quarter past seven.

8 If 1 April is a Sunday, what date is the following Thursday?

9 The scale is balanced. What is the weight of the ?

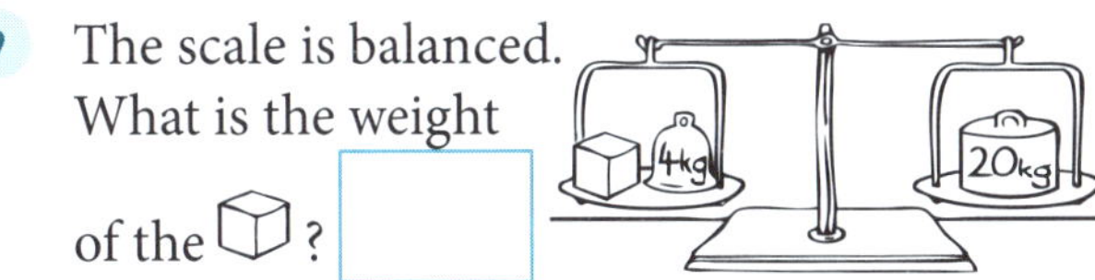

10 All four angles on a rectangle are

A the same. B different.

C sometimes the same and sometimes different.

D curved.

11 How many cubes are in the model?

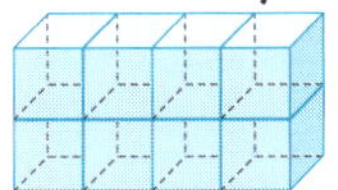

12 What shape is at D4?

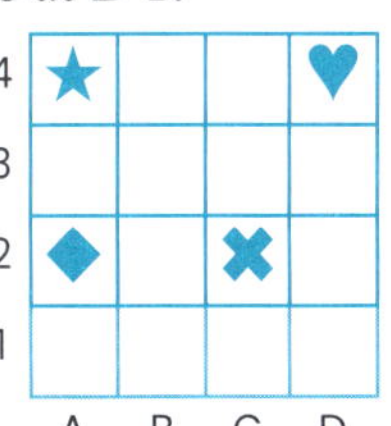

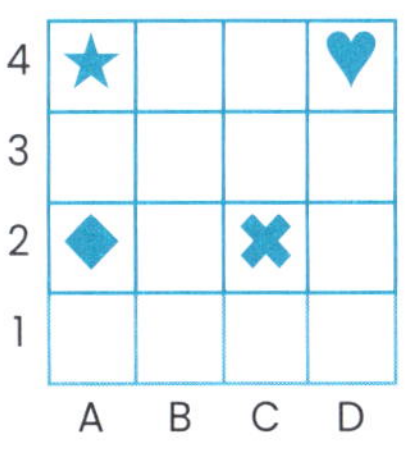

A ★ B ✖ C ◆ D 

13 Turn the rectangle a quarter turn to the left.

STATISTICS AND PROBABILITY

14 Draw the tally marks.

Books borrowed in Term 1	Tally	Total
Tilly		9
Brandon		12
George		14

School food garden

Show your working out in number sentences or drawings.

NUMBER AND ALGEBRA

1 The class grew 15 tomatoes on one plant and 12 on another plant. How many tomatoes were grown on the two plants?

2 There were 25 tomatoes on another plant. One class picked 5 tomatoes and another class picked 11.
How many tomatoes were left on the plant?

3 Year 2 bought a box of one thousand worms for their compost bin. They already had five hundred worms.
How many worms do they have now?

4 The lemon tree grew 70 lemons but Ms Smith's class picked 20 of them.
How many lemons were left on the tree?

5 There are five watermelons for ten classes. How much watermelon will each class get?

MEASUREMENT AND SPACE

6 Cherry tomatoes take about three months to grow. Baby carrots take about 50 days. Which vegetable grows faster?

7 The green waste bin can hold 470 litres of compost. If 20 more litres will fill it, how many litres of compost are in it now?

8 The school playground is a rectangle. The fence all the way around it measures 80 metres. The shorter sides are 15 metres each.

15 m 15 m

What is the length of each of the longer sides?

STATISTICS AND PROBABILITY

9 Rory mixed up the eggplant seeds with the tomato seeds. He had the same number of each kind of seed. If he plants one of the seeds, what is the chance he will grow tomatoes?

A definitely won't
B probably won't
C equal chance of growing tomatoes as eggplants
D definitely will grow tomatoes

MEASUREMENT AND SPACE

10 The class planted half of their planter box with lettuces, an eighth with carrots, an eighth with pumpkin and one quarter with tomatoes. Show on the plan how the planter box is divided.

11 a Year 6 has a vegetable garden. They have planted tomatoes and cucumbers.
What fraction of the garden bed is for tomatoes?

b When the cucumbers are finished, the class will divide that space evenly and plant spinach and lettuce instead. What fraction of the garden bed will be for the lettuce?

Tomatoes	Cucumbers

12 a Year 2 is planning a vegetable garden. The class has four things to grow equally: carrots, lettuce, spinach and zucchini. Mark and label three ways they could plant and divide their garden bed.

Option 1 Option 2 Option 3

b It takes 30 days for spinach to grow and 90 days for zucchini to grow. How many spinach crops will the class get for each zucchini crop?

c The school principal gave Year 3 a garden bed that is 1 metre wide and 1 metre long. The students will use it for carrots. They will plant the carrots 10 centimetres in from the edges and 10 centimetres apart. Use an × to mark the carrot plants on the grid.

d How many carrots can Year 3 plant in their 1-metre-by-1-metre square garden bed?

e Carrots grow in about 75 days. If the students plant the carrots on 1 September, when can they expect to pick and eat their carrots?

NUMBER AND ALGEBRA

1 Write the number that has 7 ones, 0 tens and 6 hundreds.

2 Which number is largest?

A 444
B 443
C 434
D 453

3 Which number is closest to 260?

A 266
B 220
C 250
D 26

4 Write 899 in words.

____

____

5 Write the next three numbers in the pattern.

35, 40, 45, 50, ☐, ☐, ☐

6 ◆◆◆■⊙■◆◆◆■⊙■◆◆◆■⊙■

In the pattern, how many ◆ are needed for each ⊙?

7 Write a number sentence to match the number line.

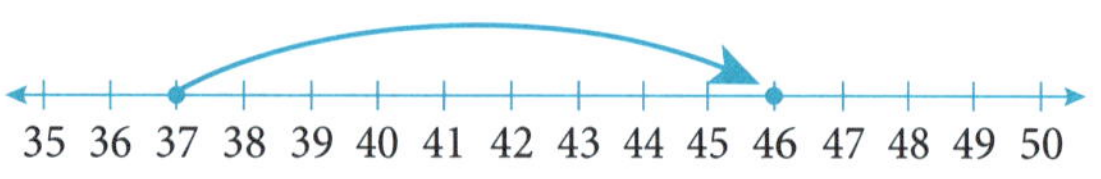

8 Complete the table.

+	50	150	250	350
350				

9 27 + 33 has the same value as

30 + ☐.

10

36 – ☐ = 27

46 – ☐ = 37

11 Nana made 20 cupcakes. Hanna took 14 to school. How many were left?

12 Lizzie had

She spent $1.50.
How much money did she have left?

13 3 + 3 + 3 + 3 + 3 + 3 is the same as

☐ × 3.

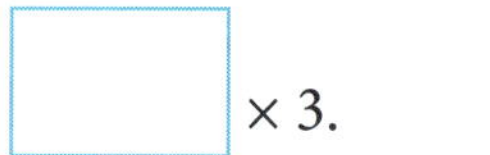

14 Five museum guides take tours with ten people each. Which one helps you work out how many people can be on tour at the same time?

A 5 + 5 + 5 + 5 + 5
B 10 + 5
C 50 ÷ 5
D 5 × 10

NUMBER AND ALGEBRA

1 Divide 60 notebooks into stacks of 10. How many stacks are there?

2 There are thirty children in the class. There are ten magazines for students to share. How many children need to share each magazine?

3 The soccer team has twelve players. They each need half an orange at half-time. How many whole oranges will need to be chopped?

4

What is the total value of the coins?

5 Monique has $5.00. How much change will she get if she buys two mangoes that cost $1.50 each?

MEASUREMENT AND SPACE

6 11:15 Write the time in words.

7 Draw hands on the clock to show quarter past six.

8 If 31 December is a Friday, what day of the week is 1 January?

9 Which unit is best to measure the length of a cricket bat?

A centimetres B metres
C kilometres D millimetres

10 All four angles on a square are

A the same. B different.
C sometimes the same and sometimes different.
D sharp.

11 Which object has no base?

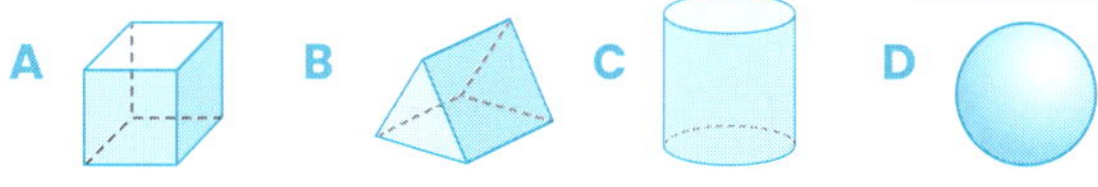

12 What object is at B2?

A  B  

C D

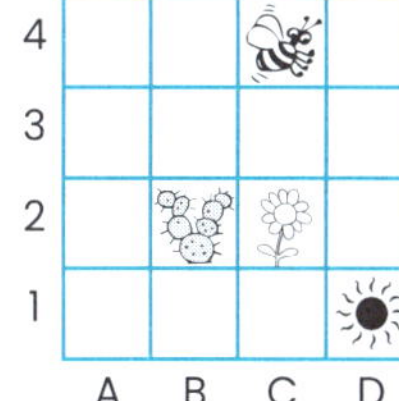

13 Flip the rectangle below the line.

STATISTICS AND PROBABILITY

14 Complete the table. Add the correct tally marks.

Books borrowed in February	Tally	Total
Jo		16
Alice		9
Misako		4

NUMBER AND ALGEBRA

1 Write the number that has four tens, three ones and five hundreds.

2 Which number is smallest?

A 204 B 240
C 420 D 402

3 Which number is closest to 660?

A 650
B 661
C 670
D 680

4 What is the value of the tens digit in 697?

5 Write the next three numbers in the pattern.

15, 25, 35, 45, ☐, ☐, ☐

6 

In the pattern, how many △ are needed for each ✣?

7 Write a number sentence to match the number line.

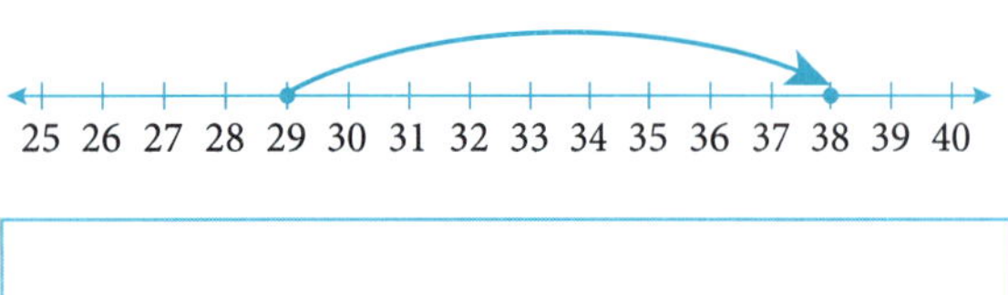

8 Complete the table.

+	50	150	250	350
550				

9 28 + 12 has the same value as

30 + ☐.

10

26 − ☐ = 19

36 − ☐ = 29

11 Phoebe had a pack of 18 jelly snakes. She gave 15 to friends. How many were left?

12 Jack had

He spent 50c. How much money did he have left?

13 6 + 6 + 6 + 6 + 6 + 6 + 6 is the same as

7 × ☐.

14 Leilani has three friends. She wants to buy six chocolate eggs for each of them. How many will she buy?

NUMBER AND ALGEBRA

1 Divide 70 notebooks into stacks of ten. How many stacks will there be?

2 Holly and Matt shared 20 pencils between them. How many did they each get?

3 Junxi cut 5 oranges into quarters. How many quarters were there?

4    

What is the total value of the coins?

5 Isla has $5.00. How much change will she get if she buys four oranges that cost $1.00 each?

MEASUREMENT AND SPACE

6 01:45 The time is quarter to

7 Draw hands on the clock to show quarter to six.

8 If 31 January is a Monday, what day of the week is 1 February?

9 Which unit is best to measure the height of a flagpole?

A centimetres B metres

C kilometres D millimetres

10 Which letter is in the triangle and the circle but not in the square?

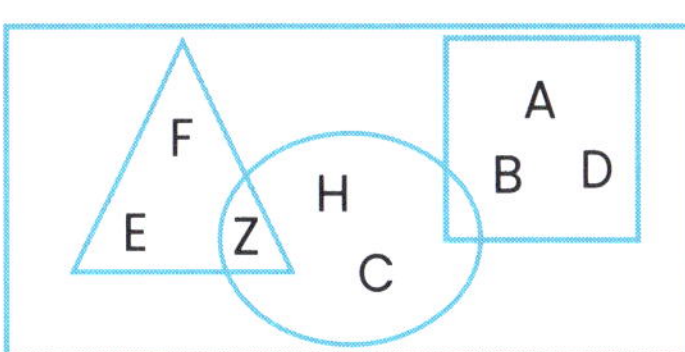

11 Which object has six faces?

A  B 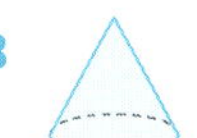 C 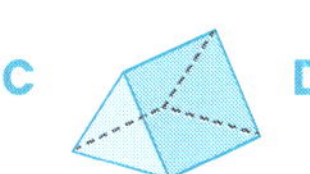 D 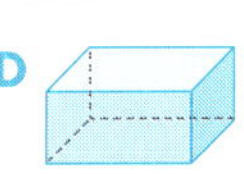

12 Draw a flower at B1 and a bee at C2.

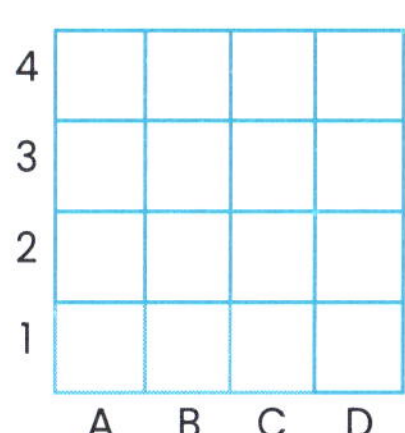

13 Flip the rectangle upwards.

STATISTICS AND PROBABILITY

14 Which fruit is most popular?

Excursion to the museum

Show your working out in number sentences or drawings.

NUMBER AND ALGEBRA

1 Twenty-four children from Year 2 went on an excursion to the museum. A teacher and five parents went with them. How many people went to the museum altogether?

2 The bus has 55 seats. How many seats were empty if there were 24 children, one teacher and five parents?

3 Twenty-four children were divided into groups of four to tour the museum. How many groups were there?

4 The 24 children were told to bring fruit for morning tea. Half of them brought apples. How many children brought apples?

5 The bus cost each child $2. How much was that altogether for 24 children?

MEASUREMENT AND SPACE

6 The bus left the school at 8:00 am and arrived at the museum at 8:30 am. How long did the bus trip take?

7 It takes 4 cups of water to fill Annie's water bottle. Each cup holds 250 millilitres. What is the capacity of her water bottle?

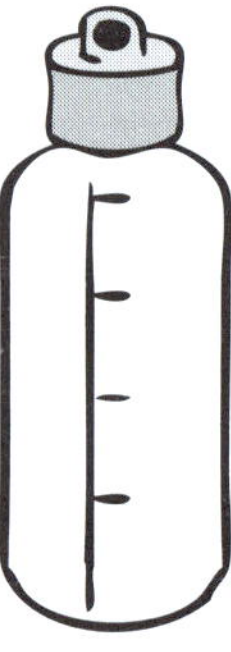

8 The bus drove west to the museum from the school. Which direction would it take to travel back to the school?

STATISTICS AND PROBABILITY

9 What are the chances of the bus getting a flat tyre on the way back to school?

A likely
B definitely will
C impossible
D unlikely

MEASUREMENT AND SPACE

This is a floor plan for Level 2 of the museum.

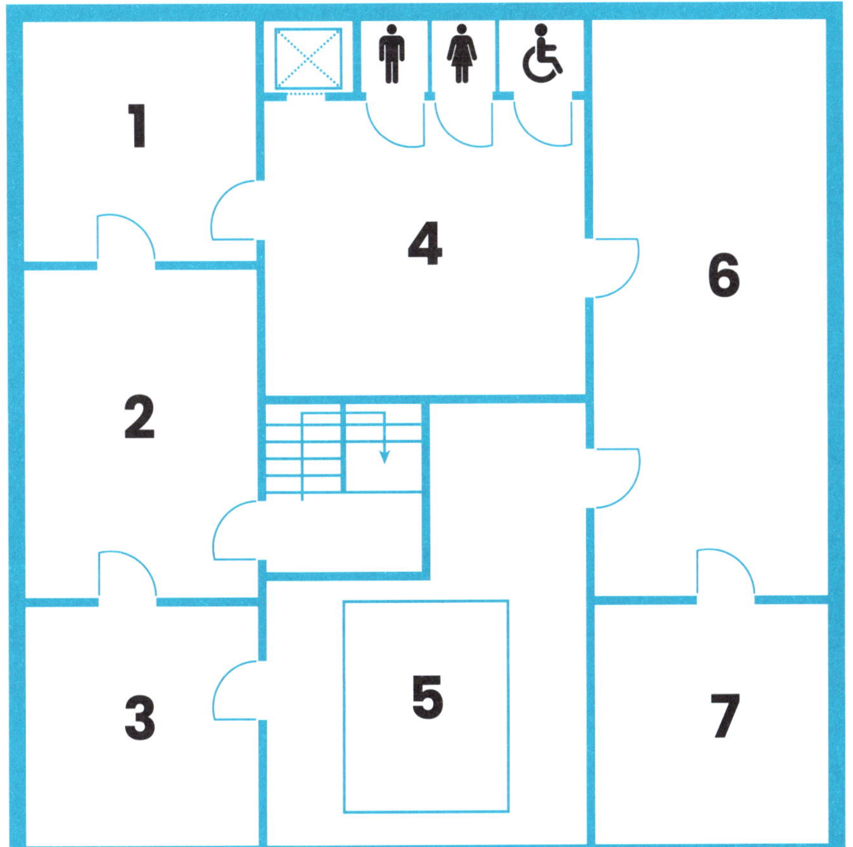

Key
Level 2

1 Dinosaur canyon: red
2 Australian fossils: blue
3 Triceratops: green
4 Muttaburrasaurus interactive exhibit: purple
5 Dinosaur life cycles: pink
6 Tyrannosaurus rex: yellow
7 Theatrette: orange

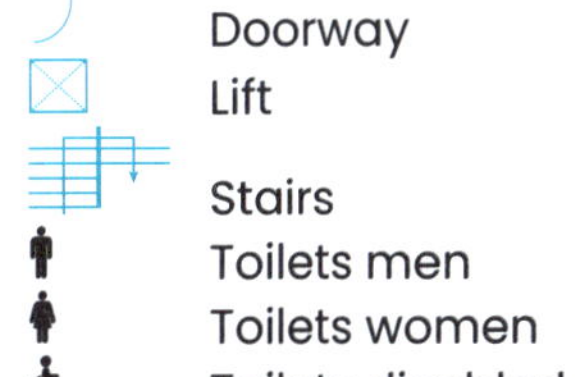

10 Colour the floor plan according to the key.

11 **a** Which two exhibits together have the same area as the Tyrannosaurus rex exhibit? ____________

b Kara's group enters level 2 via the lift. They walk through the exhibits in an anticlockwise direction. Which is the second exhibit they look at? ____________

c Which is the smallest exhibit on level 2? ____________

d Which is the largest exhibit? ____________

12 **a** Kara's group was in the theatrette when she discovered she'd left her pencils in Dinosaur canyon. Draw the quickest route she could take to get her pencils.

b Name the exhibits she walks past. ____________

NUMBER AND ALGEBRA

1 Write the number that has six tens, zero ones and three hundreds.

2 Which number is smallest?

A 149 B 139

C 129 D 159

3 Which number is closest to 700?

A 750

B 760

C 770

D 780

4 Write the number 507 in words.

____

____

5 Write the next three numbers in the pattern.

35, 45, 55, 65, ☐, ☐, ☐

6 

How many ⊙ are needed for each O?

7 Write a number sentence to match the number line.

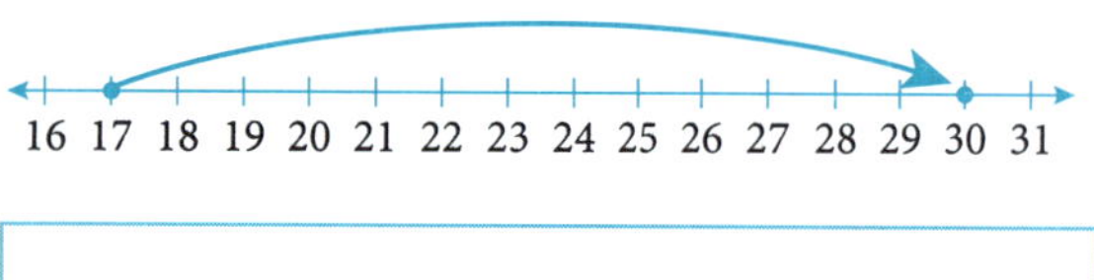

8 Complete the table.

+	50	150	250	350
650				

9

22 + 18 = 30 + ☐

66 + 14 = 70 + ☐

10

75 − ☐ = 55

85 − ☐ = 55

11 The class has 25 children but 2 were absent. How many were at school?

12 Ronan had these coins: $1, 50c, 20c. He spent $1.20. How much money did he have left?

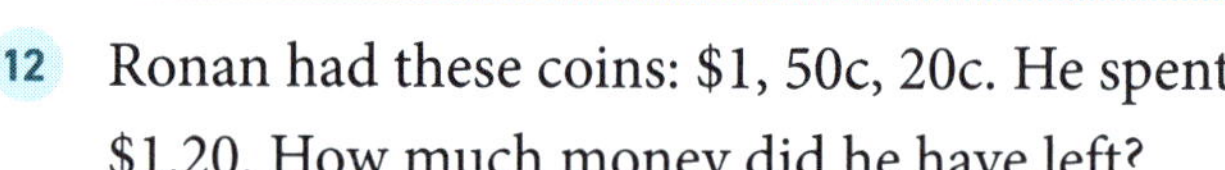

13 5 + 5 + 5 + 5 + 5 + 5 + 5 + 5 is the same as

5 × ☐.

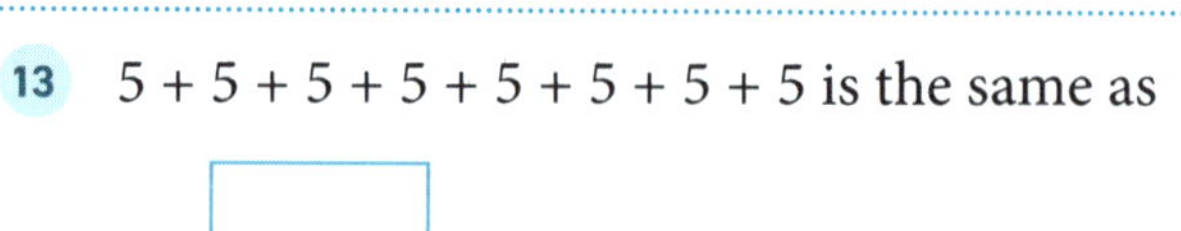

14 George washed 4 cars on Saturday. He earned $10.00 for each car. How much money did he make?

NUMBER AND ALGEBRA

1 Divide 40 into groups of 5. How many groups will you get?

2 The library ordered 50 novels for 10 children in the Reading Club. How many novels will each child get?

3 Twelve children got half an orange each. How many oranges were there?

4 How many 5c pieces are needed to make 50c?

5 Ariel has $2.40. Apples cost 50c each. How many apples can she buy?

MEASUREMENT AND SPACE

6 

Write the time in words.

The time is quarter to 

7 Draw hands on the clock to show quarter to eleven.

8 If 1 February is a Monday, what day of the week is 31 January?

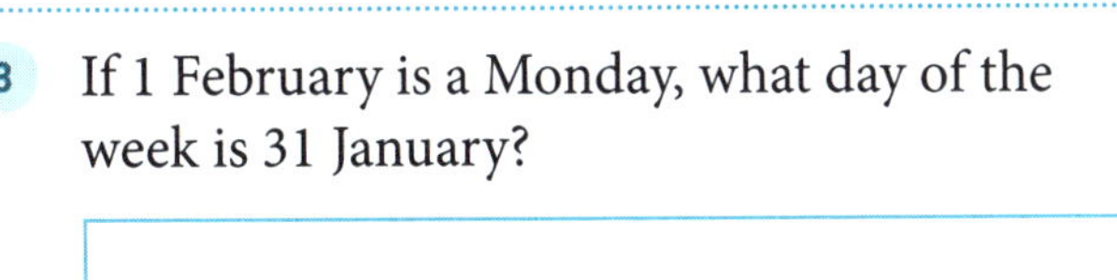

9 Which unit is best used to measure flour to make a cake?

A centimetres B grams

C millilitres D tonnes

10 Which shape has the most corners?

A  B   C  D 

11 Which object has exactly five faces?

A 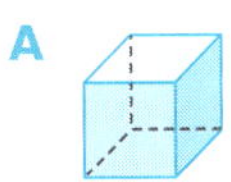 B   C 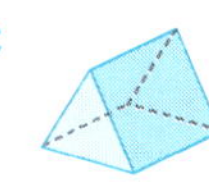 D 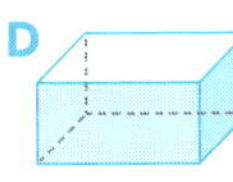

12 Draw a flower at D3 and a leaf at C2.

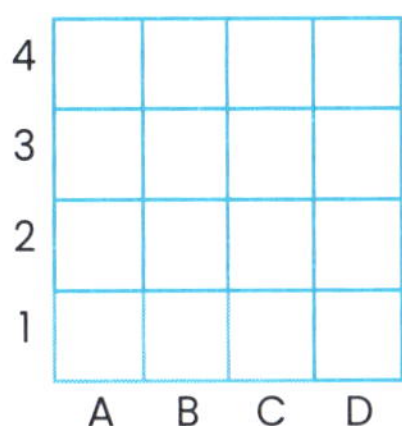

13 Slide the shaded rectangle one square to the right. Colour it in its new location.

STATISTICS AND PROBABILITY

14 Which animal is least popular?

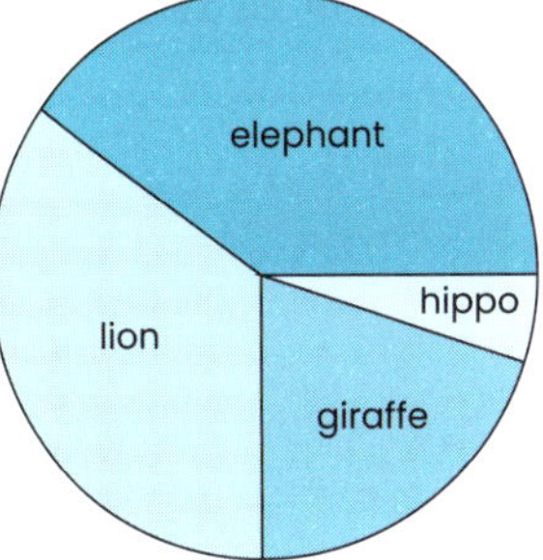

NUMBER AND ALGEBRA

1 Write the number that has six tens, five ones and zero hundreds.

2 Which number is smallest?

A 1000 B 90 C 109 D 190

3 Which number is closest to 98?

A 970
B 990
C 107
D 100

4 What is the value of the tens digit in 842?

5 Write the next three numbers in the pattern.

10, 20, 30, 40, ☐, ☐, ☐

6 Which pattern subtracts 1 each time?

A 10, 8, 6, 2 B 10, 9, 8, 7
C 13, 11, 9, 7 D 1, 2, 3, 4

7 Write a number sentence to match the number line.

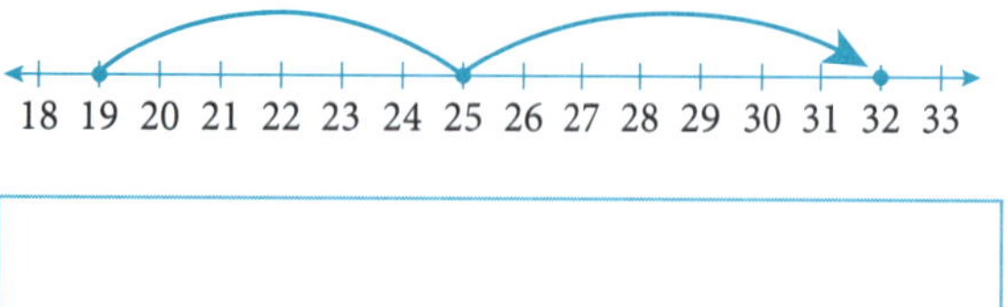

8 Complete the table.

+	50	150	250	350
50				

9

56 + 14 = 60 + ☐

75 + 25 = 80 + ☐

10

88 – ☐ = 44

66 – 33 = ☐

11 On his walk, Griffin was given 8 treats from a pack of 20 treats. How many treats were left after his walk?

12 Walter had these coins:

He spent $2.10. What change did he get?

☐

13 5 + 5 + 5 + 5 + 5 + 5 + 5 + 5 + 5

is the same as ☐ × 5.

14 Cooper bought 4 packets of muffins. Which one helps you work out how many muffins he got if there were 6 muffins in each pack?

☐

A 4 × 6 B 6 × 6 C 24 – 6 D 4 + 6

NUMBER AND ALGEBRA

1 Divide 90 into groups of 10. How many groups will you get?

2 Linda cooked 18 party pies to share with 8 other children. How many pies did each child get?

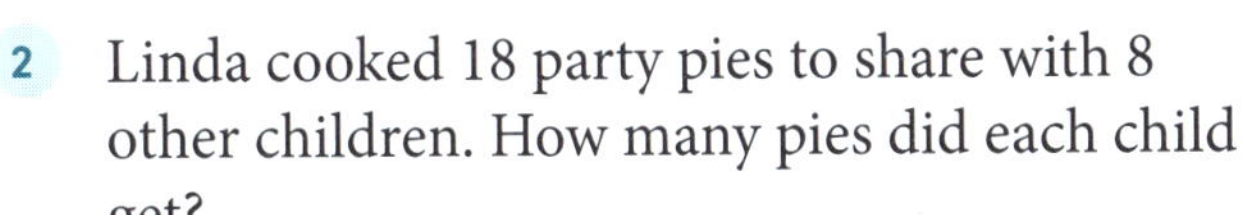

3 Ah Lam cut 6 oranges into quarters. How many quarters were there?

4

What is the total value of the coins?

5 Harper has $3.00. Muffins cost $1.50 each. How many muffins can she buy?

MEASUREMENT AND SPACE

6 06:45 The time is quarter to

7 Draw hands on the clock to show quarter to eight.

8 If 31 March is a Monday, what day of the week is 4 April?

9 Which unit is best used to measure the length of time to boil an egg?

A centimetres
B seconds
C minutes
D hours

10 Which shape has 6 corners?

A  B  C  D 

11 Which solid object has only two flat faces?

A   B 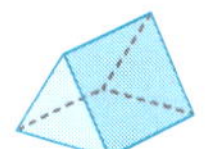  C D 

12 Colour the squares to show the quickest way for the dog to get the bone. You cannot move diagonally.

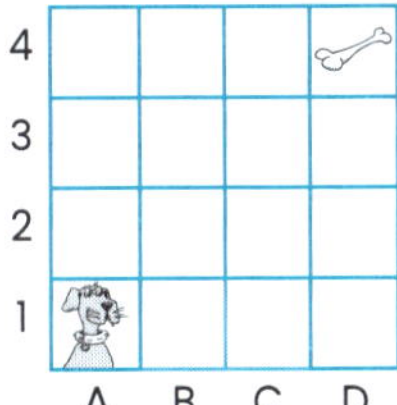

13 Slide the shaded rectangle to the left one square. Colour it in its new location.

STATISTICS AND PROBABILITY

14 Which pizza is most popular?

Favourite pizzas of 2M

Holidays and adventure

Show your working out in number sentences or drawings.

NUMBER AND ALGEBRA

1 Georgie's family will spend two weeks in Adelaide on holiday. They will drive for three days to get there and three days to get home. How long will they be away?

2 Dad drove 2 kilometres to the shop, then a further 4 kilometres to get petrol before returning to the camping ground. How far did he drive altogether?

3 Georgie is 7. Her older sister is 12. What is the age difference?

4 There are 5 people in the family. Mum packed 5 pieces of fruit for each family member. How many pieces did she pack altogether?

5 The 5 people shared 2 pizzas for dinner. Each pizza was cut into 10 slices. Dad ate 5 slices. The others ate 3 slices each. How many slices were left over?

MEASUREMENT AND SPACE

6 It's a 45-minute drive to the national park from the camping grounds. If the family leaves at eight o'clock, what time will they get to the park?

A 9:15
B 8:15
C 8:45
D 9:45

7 The family took 4 hours to hike 12 kilometres. How far did they walk each hour?

8 Dad's damper recipe needs 250 grams of flour. How much flour will he need if he doubles the recipe?

STATISTICS AND PROBABILITY

9 The family played Spotto for red cars as they drove. If they counted 86 cars before they spotted the first red car, how likely was it that the next car would be red?

A very likely
B very unlikely
C impossible
D certain

MEASUREMENT AND SPACE

10 Georgie's family live in Brisbane. They had to decide whether to holiday in Darwin or Adelaide.

a The distance from Brisbane to Darwin is three thousand, four hundred and twenty-six kilometres. This distance can be written as

A 34 206 km. **B** 30 426 km. **C** 3426 km. **D** 3406 km.

b The distance from Brisbane to Adelaide is two thousand and seven kilometres. This distance can be written as

A 207 km. **B** 20 007 km. **C** 2007 km. **D** 2700 km.

c Which journey is the shorter distance?

A Brisbane to Darwin **B** Brisbane to Adelaide

11 Here is a map of the camping ground and caravan park where Georgie's family stayed.

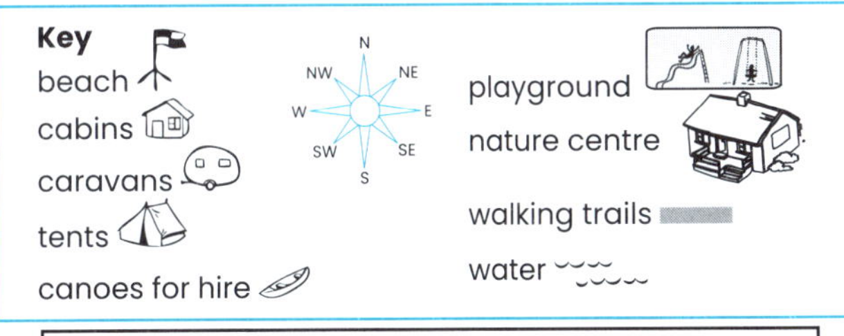

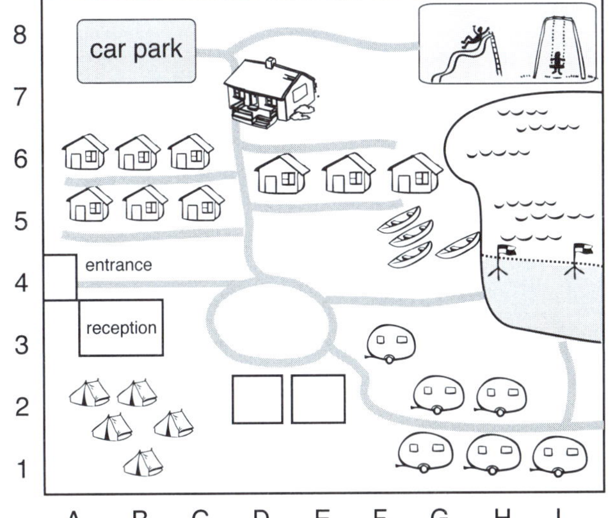

a Colour the water blue.

b Georgie's family parked their caravan at I1. Colour their caravan red.

c Georgie made friends with a child in the caravan at G2. Colour that caravan orange.

d Label the showers at D2 with S and the toilets at E2 with T.

e To get to the beach Georgie needs to walk

A north. **B** south.

C east. **D** west.

f In which direction is the playground from Georgie's caravan?

12 Friends are visiting Georgie's family at the caravan park. Write the instructions she will give them to meet her at the playground. They will enter by car and park in the car park, then walk to the playground. ______________________________

____

NUMBER AND ALGEBRA

1 Which of these is 521?

A 500 + 10 + 20
B 100 + 20 + 5
C 5 + 2 + 1
D 500 + 20 + 1

2 Which number is largest?

A 90 B 900 C 100 D 1000

3 Which number is closest to 80?

A 97 B 99 C 91 D 98

4 What is the value of the ones digit in 290?

5 Circle the odd numbers.

0 1 2 3 4 5 6 7 8 9 10

6 Which pattern shows the numbers doubling?

A 2, 4, 6, 8
B 2, 4, 8, 16
C 1, 2, 3, 4
D 2, 5, 11, 23

7 Write a number sentence to match the number line.

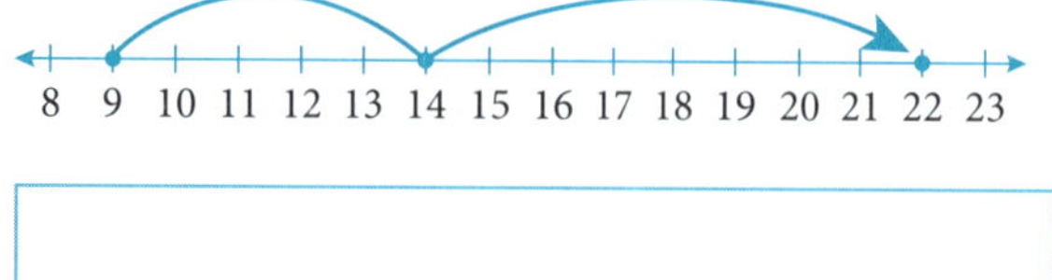

8 Complete the table.

+	50	150	250	350
25				

9

56 + 15 = 60 + ☐

75 + 26 = 100 + ☐

10

21 – 11 = ☐

31 – 11 = ☐

11 The library had 15 books on its 'HOT READS' shelf. Maggie borrowed 3. How many were left on the shelf?

12 Gian had 

He bought an eraser for $1.60. Did he have enough money left to buy a pencil for $1.30?

13 3 + 3 + 3 + 3 + 3 + 3 is the same as

 × 3.

14 Carla bought 6 packets of muffins. There were 6 muffins in each pack.

How many muffins did she get?

A 6 + 6
B 6 × 6
C 6 + 6 + 6 + 6
D 6 – 6

NUMBER AND ALGEBRA

1 Divide 60 into groups of 5. How many groups will you get?

2 There are 20 apples for 5 donkeys. How many apples will each donkey get?

3 Charlie ate one-quarter of an orange. Which fraction of the orange was left?

A $\frac{1}{2}$ B $\frac{3}{4}$ C $\frac{1}{3}$ D $\frac{1}{8}$

4 How many 10c coins are needed to make $1?

5 Phoebe has 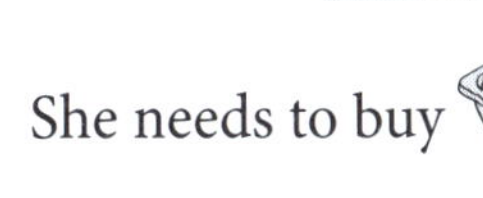.

She needs to buy 

Does she have enough money?

MEASUREMENT AND SPACE

6 It's now quarter to six. Timmy needs to get out of bed in fifteen minutes. Write the numbers on the digital clock to show the time he will get up.

7 The quiche will be cooked in fifteen minutes. The time will be

A 12:00 B 11:45 C 12:15 D 11:00

8 If 26 March is a Thursday, what day and date is the last day in March?

9 Which object has the greatest capacity?

A 

B 

C 

D

10 This shape has ☐ corners and ☐ sides.

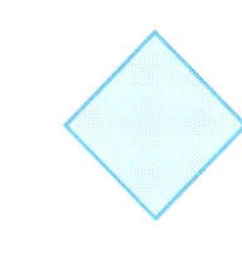

11 Which object has 6 surfaces and 8 corners?

A 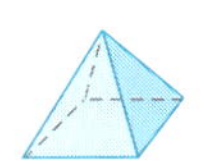 B 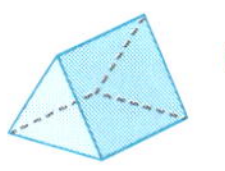 C D 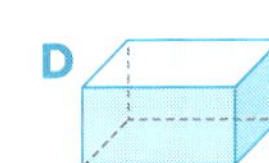

12 Draw the path to show the longest route between the wombat (W) and its tunnel (T). Do not move diagonally. How many squares did the wombat cross?

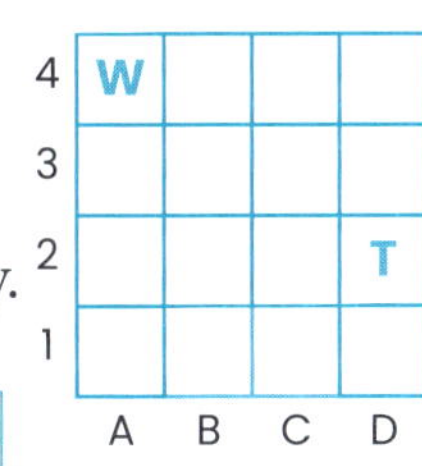

13 Draw the shape a quarter turn to the left.

STATISTICS AND PROBABILITY

14 Complete the column graph. Three children only have a dog. Four children only have a cat. One child has two mice and two dogs. Draw the pets on the graph.

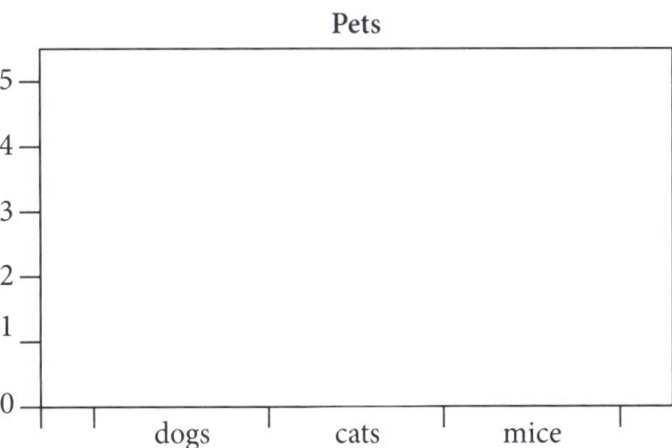

NUMBER AND ALGEBRA

1 Which of these is 730?

A 700 + 300 + 0 B 700 + 30 + 0
C 7 + 3 + 1 D 70 + 3

2 Which number is largest?

A 877 B 90
C 876 D 98

3 Which number is closest to 500?

A 900 B 600 C 590 D 510

4 What is the value of the tens digit in 345?

5 Write the next three numbers in the pattern.

75, 65, 55, 45, ___, ___, ___

6 Which pattern adds 4 each time?

A 12, 15, 18 B 18, 24, 30
C 18, 22, 26 D 6, 8, 10

7 Write a number sentence to match the number line.

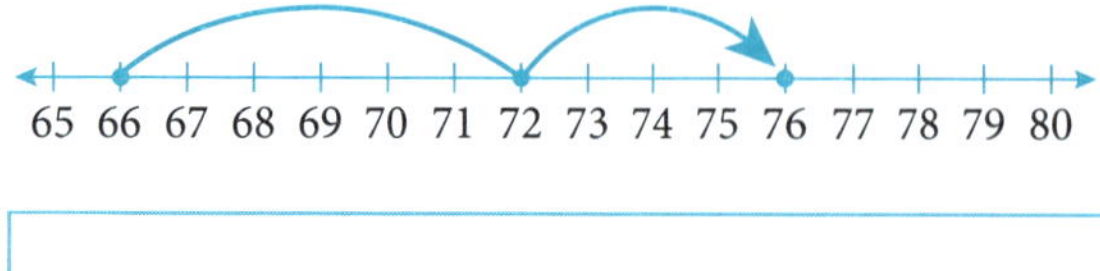

8 Complete the table.

+	150	250	350	450
20				

9

36 + 18 = 40 + ___

35 + 27 = 50 + ___

10

32 – 12 = ___

42 – 12 = ___

11 There are 14 children on the team but 2 children were absent for training on Monday. How many children attended training on Monday?

12 Jayden had  

He bought an apple for $1.20. How much change did he get?

13 5 + 5 + 5 + 5 + 5 + 5 + 5 + 5 + 5

is the same as 9 × ___.

14 Isabella bought 4 bags of chocolate. There were 22 chocolates in each bag. How many chocolates did she get?

NUMBER AND ALGEBRA

1 How many 5s are in 70?
Tip: count by 5s to 70.

2 There are 30 carrots to be packed into bags of 10. How many bags will there be?

3 Which one shows $\frac{1}{4}$?

A  B  C  D 

4 How many 20c coins are needed to make $1?

5 Lexi has 

She needs to buy 

Does she have enough money?

MEASUREMENT AND SPACE

6 It's now quarter to seven in the morning. Jay needs to get out of bed in fifteen minutes. Draw the numbers on the digital clock to show the time he will get up.

7 How many lots of five minutes are there in an hour?
Tip: count by 5s to 60.

8 ANZAC Day is 25 April.
What day of the week is ANZAC Day if the Saturday before is 23 April?

9 Which object has the greatest capacity?

10 Colour the shapes which have four equal angles.

11 Which object has no corners?

12 The star is at B1 and the sun is at D4.
Draw a moon at A4.

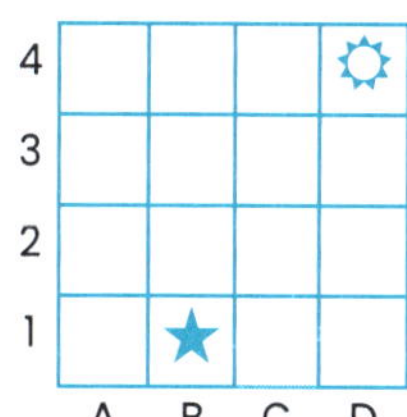

13 Flip the triangle over the line and draw it.

STATISTICS AND PROBABILITY

14 Five children chose chocolate. Three children chose strawberry. One child chose vanilla. Complete the column graph.

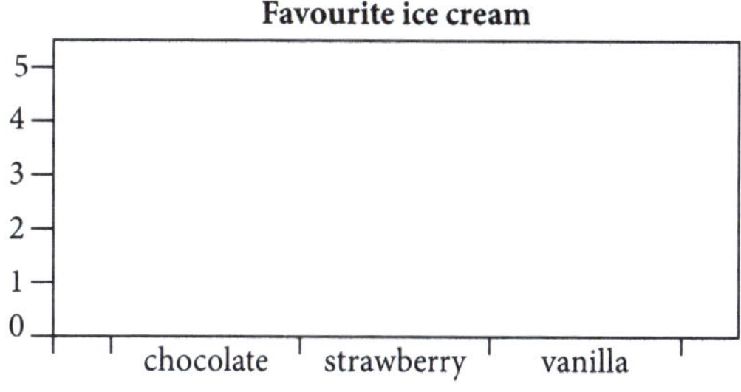

Money

Show your working out in number sentences or drawings.

NUMBER AND ALGEBRA

1 Students donated a gold coin for charity on mufti day. Twenty children gave $1 and ten children gave $2. How much was donated altogether?

2 Mitchell had $20.00 to buy groceries. He spent $18.00. How much did he have left?

3 Nan gave 4 grandchildren $5 each for their piggy banks. How much money did Nan give away?

4 Harper was paid $10 for washing the car. Her brother helped so she gave him half the money. How much did she have left?

5 

Divide the money evenly between 3 children. How much will each child get?

MEASUREMENT AND SPACE

6 Sebastian earns $5.00 an hour helping his dad. How much did he earn if he started at 9 am and finished at 4 pm?

7 It took Gemma 45 minutes to add up the money in her piggy bank. She started at 2:00. Draw hands on the clock to show the time she finished.

8 Zeke walks 2 kilometres west to get to the bank. In which direction will he walk home from the bank?

STATISTICS AND PROBABILITY

9 Jackie tossed a coin 8 times. It came up heads once and tails 7 times. What is most likely to turn up next?

A heads

B tails

C Both have an equal chance.

NUMBER AND ALGEBRA

10 a Draw the coins you would use to make $2.00 using the fewest coins possible.

b Draw the coins you would use to make $2 using the largest number of coins possible.

11 a Draw 5c pieces to make $1.

b Draw 10c pieces to make $1.

c Draw 10c pieces to make $2.

d Draw 50c pieces to make $2.

12 Name the animals on the coins.

5 c	10c	20c	50c

NUMBER AND ALGEBRA

1 Which of these is 304?

A 300 + 40 + 0 B 30 + 4
C 300 + 4 D 3 + 0 + 4

2 Which number is largest?

A 790
B 760
C 97
D 107

3 Which number is closest to 601?

A 609
B 620
C 610
D 604

4 What is the value of the tens digit in 870?

5 Fill in the missing numbers in the pattern.

3, ___, ___, ___, 15, 18, 21

6 Which pattern adds 3 each time?

A 18, 24, 30, 36 B 13, 23, 33, 43
C 6, 8, 10, 12 D 12, 15, 18, 21

7

28 + ___ = 30

38 + ___ = 40

8 Complete the table.

+	170	270	370	470
25				

9

82 + 12 = 90 + ___

46 = 40 + ___

10

43 − 13 = ___ 53 − 13 = ___

11 Show 74 − 18 on the number line.

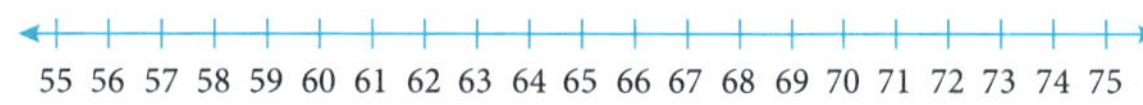

12 Riku has  

Does he have enough money to buy a loaf of bread for $3.50?

13 8 + 8 + 8 + 8 + 8 + 8 + 8

is the same as 7 × ___.

14 Toni bought 2 loaves of bread. Each loaf had 22 slices. How many slices did she get?

NUMBER AND ALGEBRA

1 How many 5s are in 65?

2 There are 100 apples in a crate. They need to be packed into bags of 10. How many bags will there be?

3 Suri ate three pieces of an orange. Which fraction of the orange did she eat?

A $\frac{1}{2}$ B $\frac{3}{4}$ C $\frac{1}{3}$ D $\frac{2}{8}$

4 What is the total value of the money?

5 Lachlan has 

He needs to buy 

Does he have enough money?

MEASUREMENT AND SPACE

6 Sean leaves for soccer training at quarter to four. Write the numbers on the digital clock to show the time he goes to training.

:

7 Monique got home fifteen minutes ago at quarter to five. Draw the hands on the clock to show the time now.

8 Which object is longer than 1 metre?

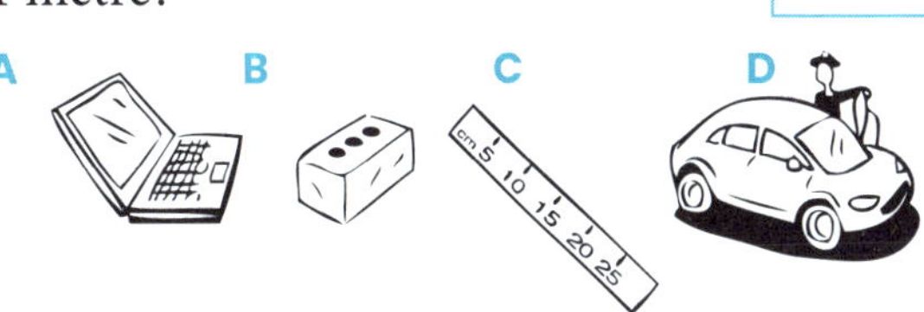

9 If 26 May is a Thursday, what day and date is the last day in May?

10 Describe this shape.

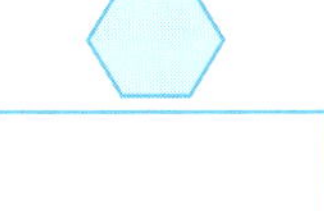

11 Draw the top view of this model.

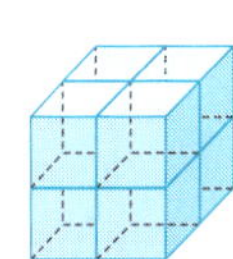

12 Which triangle is next?

A  B  C D

13 Flip the moon shape over the dotted line. Draw it.

STATISTICS AND PROBABILITY

14 Five children chose apples. Four children chose oranges. Three children chose bananas. One child chose pears. Draw the results on the graph. Which fruit is least popular?

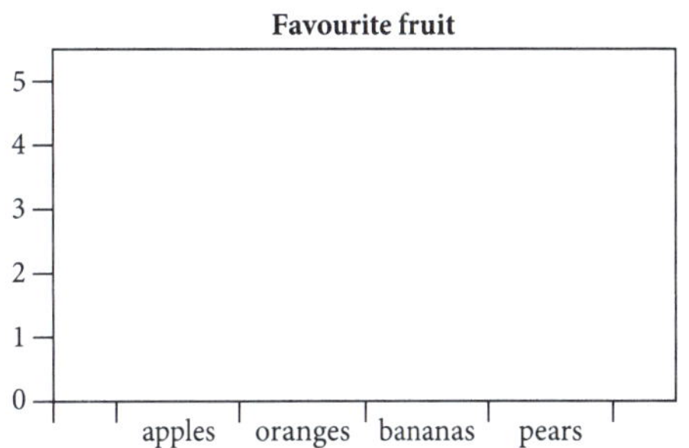

NUMBER AND ALGEBRA

1 Which of these is 682?

A 60 + 80 + 2
B 6 hundreds + 2 tens + 8 ones
C 6 + 8 + 2
D 6 hundreds + 8 tens + 2 ones

2 Which number is largest?

A 105 B 125
C 215 D 1005

3 Which number is closest to 299?

A 200 B 300
C 900 D 29

4 What is the value of the ones digit in 543?

5 Fill in the missing numbers in the pattern.

95, 90, 85,  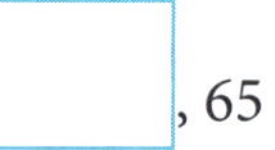 , , , 65

6 Which pattern adds 5 each time?

A 5, 11, 17, 23
B 15, 25, 35, 45
C 3, 6, 9, 12
D 11, 16, 21, 26

7

19 + ☐ = 29

29 + ☐ = 49

8 Complete the table.

+	160	260	360	460
25				

9

45 + 16 = 50 + ☐

45 + 11 = 50 + ☐

10

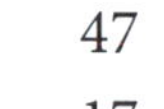

  47
– 17

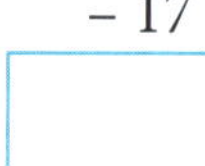

  57
– 17

11 The chickens laid 18 eggs. Mum gave 12 to the neighbours. How many eggs were left?

12 Sho has

Does he have enough money to buy a packet of bread rolls for $2.40?

13 12 + 12 + 12 + 12 + 12 + 12 + 12

is the same as ☐ × 12.

14 Frankie bought 3 loaves of bread. Each loaf had 22 slices. Write a number sentence to show how many slices he got altogether.

NUMBER AND ALGEBRA

1 Divide 22 into groups of 2. How many groups will you get?

2 There are 50 oranges in a crate. They need to be packed into bags of 5 oranges. How many bags will there be?

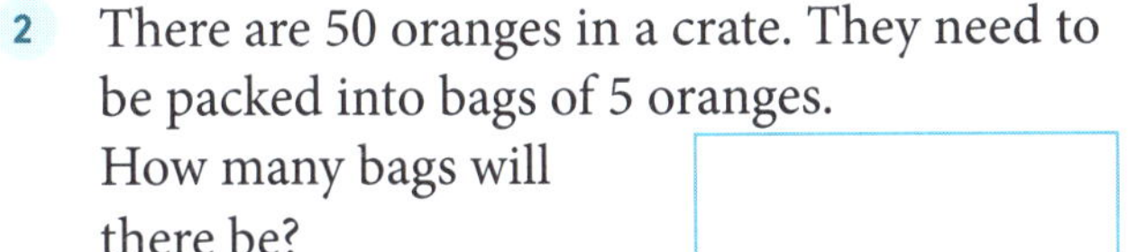

3 Melanie sliced an apple into eight even pieces. She ate three of the pieces. Which fraction of the apple did she eat?

A $\frac{1}{2}$ B $\frac{3}{4}$ C $\frac{2}{8}$ D $\frac{3}{8}$

4

What is the total value of the money?

5 James has

He needs to buy

Fish Food $4.50

How much money will he have left?

MEASUREMENT AND SPACE

6 03:45

Charlie has a ukulele lesson in 15 minutes.

Draw the numbers on the digital clock to show the time she starts her lesson.

7 It's now 6:15. Marcus has to be home in half an hour. Draw the hands on the clock to show the time Marcus will be home.

8 1 October is a Monday. What day of the week is 8 October?

9 Which object is about 1 metre in length?

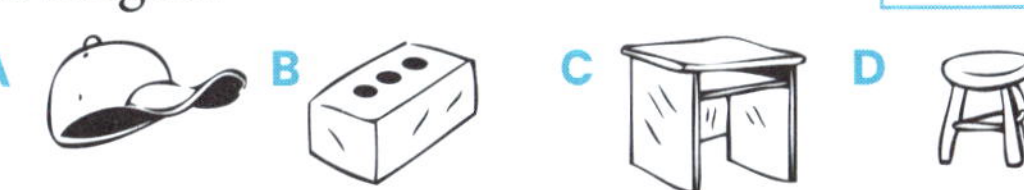

A B C D

10 This object is

A a pentagon. B an octagon.
C a triangle. D a hexagon.

11 How many edges does this object have?

12 Draw the last card.

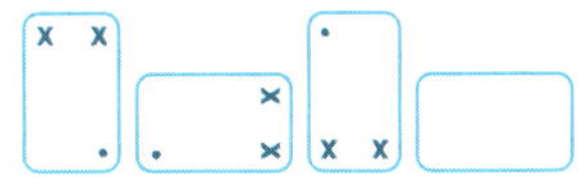

13 Which would be the image of the arrow if it is flipped over the dotted line?

A B C D

STATISTICS AND PROBABILITY

14 Five children chose whales, six children chose dolphins and three children chose dugongs. Draw the results on the graph.

Which animal is the most popular?

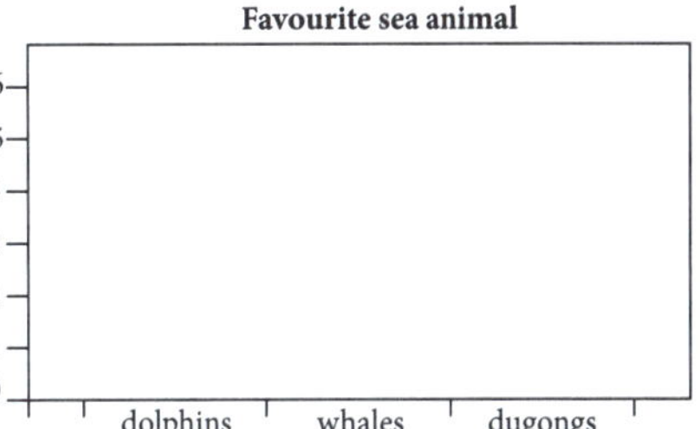

Let's cook

Show your working out in number sentences or drawings.

NUMBER AND ALGEBRA

1 Sally and Vince are making a Vietnamese stir-fry. The recipe is for two people. It uses 200 grams of tofu. If they are feeding four people, how much tofu will they need?

2 The children have a 100-gram bag of cashews but only need 65 grams for the recipe. How many grams of cashews will be left over?

3 The recipe is for two people. If Sally and Vince want to feed ten people, what should they multiply the ingredients by?

4 The recipe uses 250 grams of noodles for two people. How many grams of noodles does each person get?

5 The tofu costs $2.50, the noodles cost $1.50 and the cashews cost $1.80. How much did those ingredients cost?

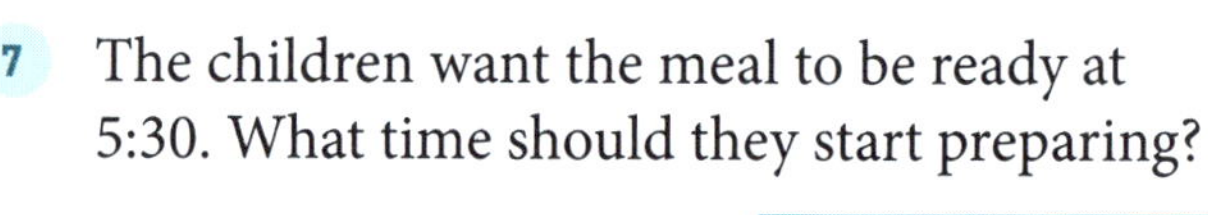

MEASUREMENT AND SPACE

6 It will take 15 minutes to prepare the ingredients and 15 minutes to cook the recipe. If the children start preparing at 5:30, what time will the stir-fry be ready to eat?

7 The children want the meal to be ready at 5:30. What time should they start preparing?

8 The tofu comes in a block that is 5 cm by 3 cm by 2 cm. Which picture shows what the block of tofu would look like without its packaging?

A
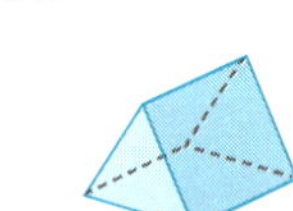

B

C
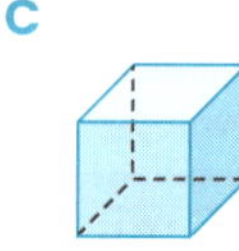

D
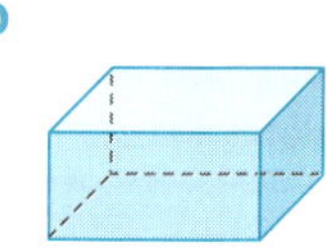

STATISTICS AND PROBABILITY

9 Sally and Vince are usually successful when they cook. What is the likelihood of the stir-fry being a success?

A likely B unlikely
C certain D impossible

STATISTICS AND PROBABILITY

Sally's class had a bake-off competition. The graph shows how many children voted for each of the top five cakes.

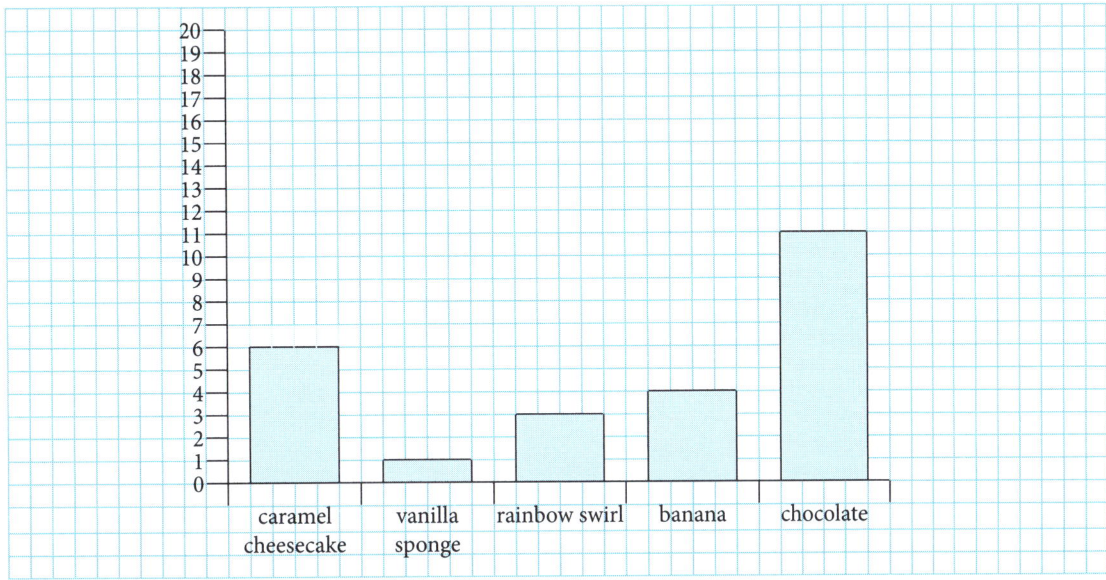

10 a Which cake is most popular? ______

b Which cake is least popular? ______

c Which cake would likely sell the best at a fete? ______

d The cheesecake ingredients cost $12. The chocolate cake ingredients cost half as much. How much do the chocolate cake ingredients cost? ______

e How many children voted altogether? ______

11 Ask your classmates or family members to vote for their favourite cake or other food. Try to find at least ten people to vote. Draw a graph to show the results.

12 Answer the questions below about your graph.

a Which food is most popular with your group of voters? ______

b Which food is least popular? ______

c How many people voted? ______

NUMBER AND ALGEBRA

1 Which of these is 860?

A $8 + 6 + 0$

B $800 + 60 + 0$

C $8 + 6$

D $80 + 60$

2 What number is exactly halfway between 245 and 295?

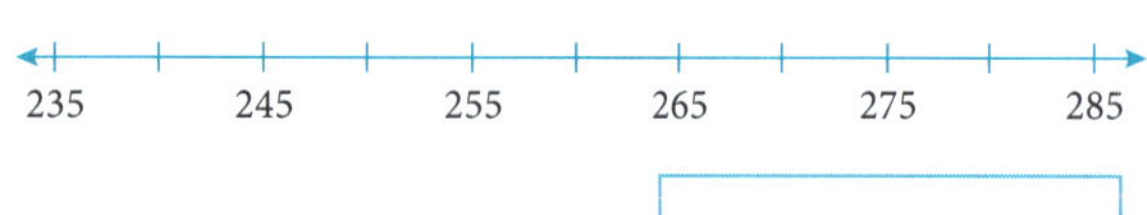

3 Tia's book has more than 200 pages but less than 220. How many pages might the book have?

A 210 B 200

C 228 D 221

4 What is the value of the tens digit in 435?

5 This pattern adds 7. Fill in the missing numbers.

7, ☐, ☐, ☐, 35, 42

6 Which pattern goes backwards by 5 each time?

A 100, 90, 80, 70

B 45, 39, 33, 27

C 42, 37, 32, 27

D 55, 45, 35, 25

7

$18 + \square = 38$

$28 + \square = 48$

8 Complete the table.

+	170	270	370	470
20				

9

$44 + 18 = 50 + \square$

$59 + 11 = 60 + \square$

10

$66 - 16 = \square$

$76 - 16 = \square$

11 Dad cooked 16 pancakes. The family ate 14. How many were left over?

12 The class planted 20 trees. Fifteen were along the fence. The rest were near the gate. How many were near the gate?

13 $8 + 8 + 8 + 8 + 8 + 8 + 8$

is the same as $\square \times 8$.

14 Joe needs to make 20 sandwiches for a party. Write a number sentence to show how many slices of bread he will need.

NUMBER AND ALGEBRA

1 Divide 30 into groups of 2. How many groups will you get?

2 The florist has 120 tulips to be divided into bunches of 12. How many bunches will there be?

3 A chocolate bar has eight segments. Billy ate five segments. Which fraction of the chocolate did he eat?

A 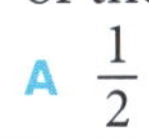 $\frac{1}{2}$ B 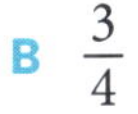 $\frac{3}{4}$ C  $\frac{5}{8}$ D $\frac{8}{5}$

4 Tayla has

Does she have enough money to buy four bread rolls for 55c each?

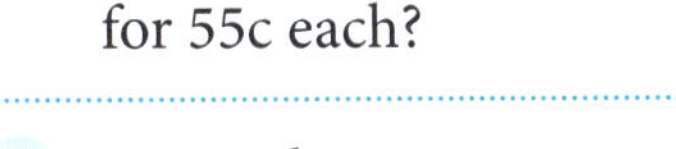

5 Jeremy has

He buys

How much money does he have left?

MEASUREMENT AND SPACE

6 It is half past four. Maxine needs to be home in half an hour. Draw the hands on the clock to show the time she needs to be home.

7 The lunch bell will ring in 15 minutes, at one o'clock.
What time is it now?

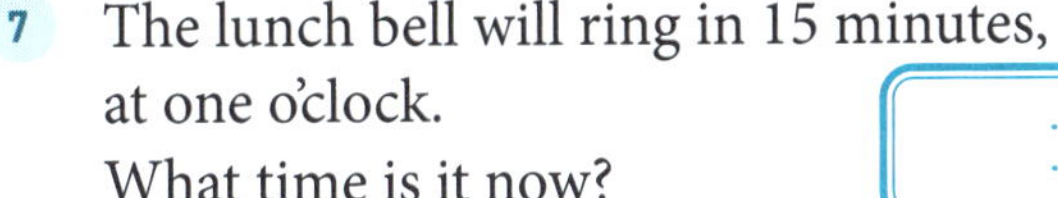

8 31 August is a Friday. What day of the week is 2 September?

9 Which answer has an area of 3 square units?

A B C D

10 Name the shape at the top of this object.

11 Draw the top view of this object.

12 Draw the pattern on the last card.

13 Draw the other half of the symmetrical shape.

STATISTICS AND PROBABILITY

14 Seven children chose bees, six chose beetles and four chose grasshoppers.

Draw the results on the graph.

Which insect is the most popular?

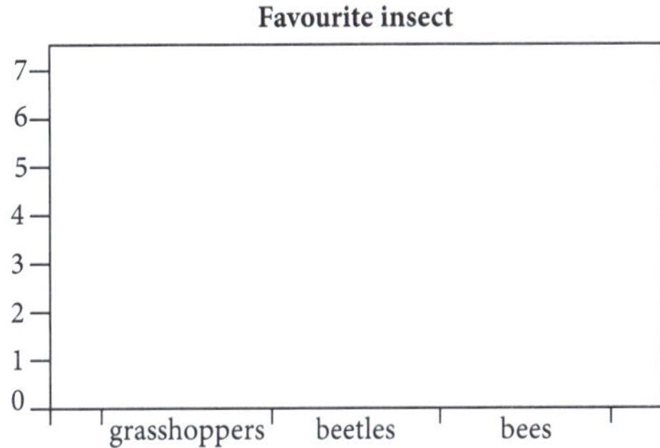

NUMBER AND ALGEBRA

1 Which of these is 610?

A 600 + 10 + 1 B 600 + 100

C 600 + 10 + 0 D 61 + 0

2 Write the largest number you can make from the digits 6, 0 and 9.

3 Write the smallest number you can make from the digits 0, 2 and 1.

4 What number is exactly halfway between 160 and 220?

150 160 170 180 190 200 210 220

5 Fill in the missing numbers in the pattern.

45, 41, ___, ___, ___, 25, 21, 17

6 Which pattern goes backwards by 10 each time?

A 62, 53, 44, 35

B 50, 60, 70, 80

C 92, 82, 72, 62

D 55, 50, 45, 40

7

20 + ___ = 38

30 + ___ = 48

8 Complete the table.

+	170	270	370	470
30				

9

23 + 17 = 30 + ___

15 + 45 = 50 + ___

10 Complete the table.

+	60	70	80	90
30				

11 Write a number sentence to match the number line.

67 68 69 70 71 72 73 74 75 76 77 78 79 80 81 82 83 84 85 86 87

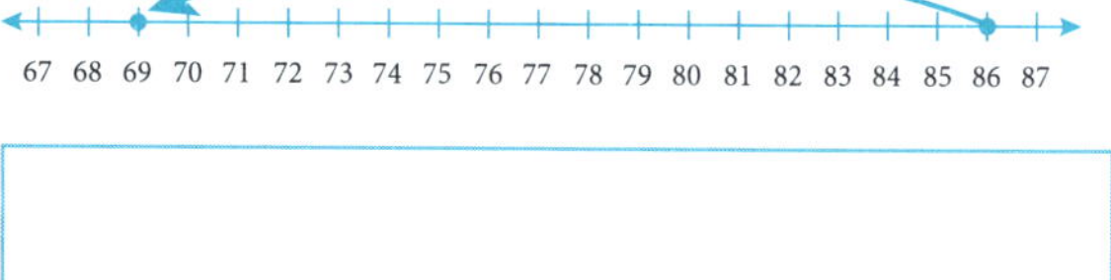

12 Dad bought 25 grevilleas. He planted 16 on Saturday and the rest on Sunday. How many did he plant on Sunday?

13 12 + 12 + 12 + 12 + 12 + 12 + 12 + 12 + 12

is the same as ___ × 12.

14 Robbie is making pancake stacks. He needs five stacks of three pancakes. Write a number sentence to show how many pancakes he needs to make for all his stacks.

NUMBER AND ALGEBRA

1 Divide 45 into groups of 5. How many groups will you get?

2 120 golf balls will be sold in bags of 10. How many bags will there be?

3 Which one shows $\frac{1}{8}$?

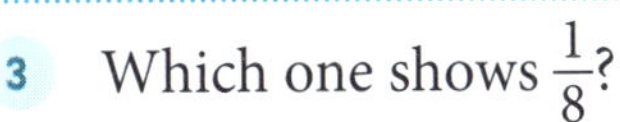

4

What is the total value of the money?

5 Jasmine has

She needs to buy

How much money will she have left?

MEASUREMENT AND SPACE

6 Amanda should have been home at three o'clock but she was half an hour late. What time did she get home?

7 Maddie has thirty minutes for reading. It is now two o'clock. What time will she need to stop reading?

8 1 August is a Friday. What day of the week is 31 July?

9
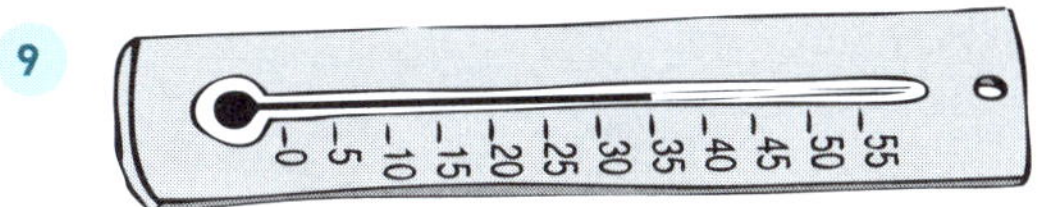

What is the temperature?

Is it a good temperature for swimming at the beach?

10 Draw the other half of the cat's face.

11 Describe this object.

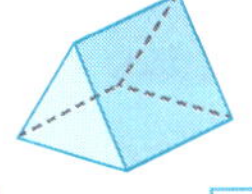

☐ surfaces ☐ vertices ☐ edges

12 Draw the spots on the last card.

13 Which shapes are the same on each side of the dotted lines?

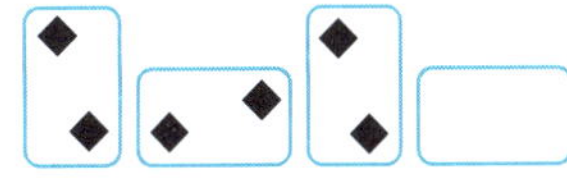

STATISTICS AND PROBABILITY

14 Complete the column graph.
Eight children chose penguins, four chose eagles, one chose owls and one chose lorikeets. Draw the results on the graph.
Which animal is the most popular?

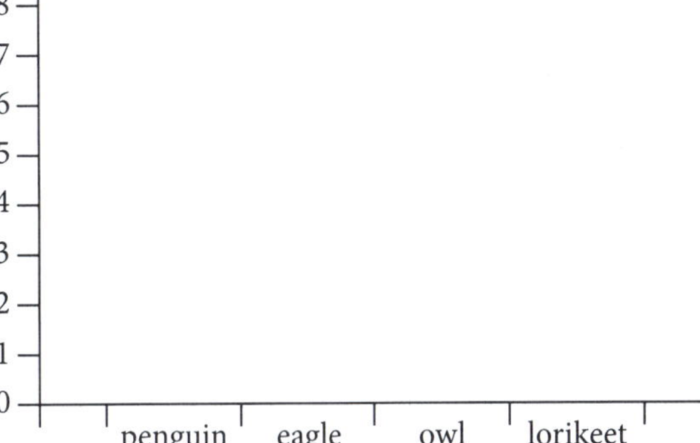

At school

Show your working out in number sentences or drawings.

NUMBER AND ALGEBRA

1 Class 2K has 14 boys and 13 girls. How many children are in 2K?

2 Twenty-eight children were in the library. Sixteen were using computers. The rest were reading books. How many people were reading books?

3 Lauren has four times as many pencils as Max. Max has five pencils. How many does Lauren have?

4 Karla, Billy and Jayne share some pencils. Each child got six pencils. How many pencils were there altogether?

5 The school raised money to help wildlife. 2W raised \$22.50 and 2J raised \$36.40. How much money did the two classes raise altogether?

MEASUREMENT AND SPACE

6 Sarah helped the teacher mix glue for papier-mâché. They needed 10 litres. How many 2-litre jugs will it take to fill the 10-litre bucket?

7 Bill weighs just over 26 kilograms. When he lifts a shot-put, he weighs nearly 29 kilograms. What is the approximate weight of the shot-put?

8 Neri lives two kilometres east of her school. Jacob lives two and a half kilometres further east. How far is Jacob from their school?

STATISTICS AND PROBABILITY

9 The teacher asked the class to vote to decide which novel to read next. *Matilda* won the vote. How likely is it that the teacher will read *Matlida* to the class?

A certain B likely
C unlikely D impossible

STATISTICS AND PROBABILITY

Class 2H needs to choose a colour for their class team in the school charity walk. The teacher recorded the students' choices in a table using tally marks.

Colour	Tally	Result
red		
blue	𝍸 ||||	
yellow	𝍸	
orange	|	
green	|||	
purple	||	
pink	||||	

10 Add the tally marks and fill in the Result column.

11 Answer the questions.

a Based on the results in the table, which colour should be used for the class team?

b Which colour is the least popular?

12 a Show the results of the class tally in this column graph. Write the names of the colours on the horizontal axis. Write numbers on the vertical axis. Colour the columns appropriately.

b How many more students like blue than red?

c Which colour is the second favourite?

d Does the column graph make it easier or harder to read the data and answer questions about the results? Why?

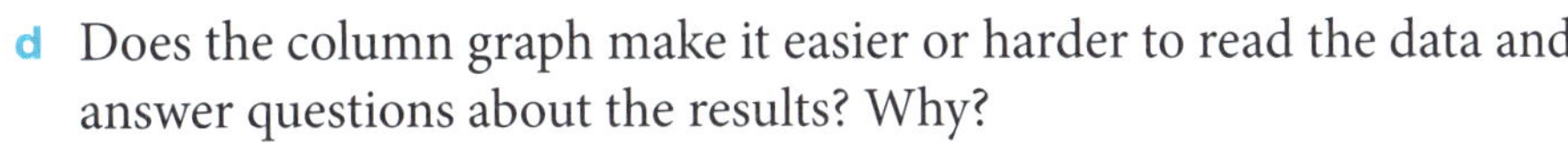

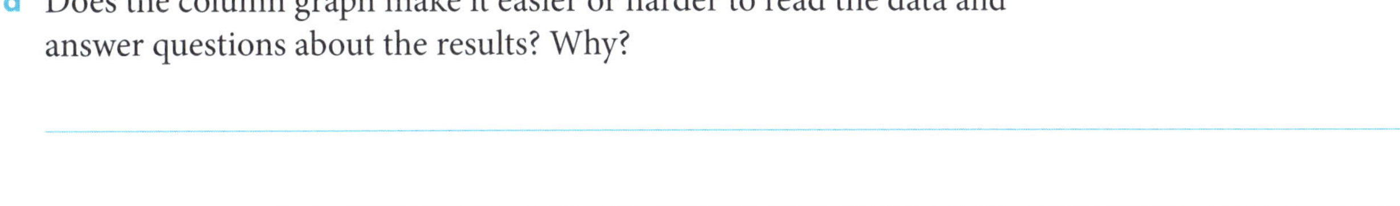

NUMBER AND ALGEBRA

1 Which of these is 802?

A 800 + 20
B 800 + 100 + 2
C 800 + 2
D 82 + 0

2 Which number is largest?

A 99 B 901
C 999 D 91

3 Write the largest number you can make from the digits 1, 7 and 3.

4 What number is exactly halfway between 130 and 210?

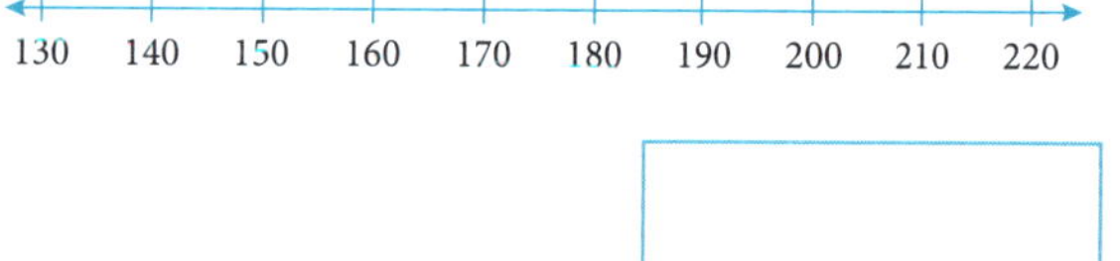

5 Fill in the missing numbers in the pattern.

56, 54, 52, ☐, ☐, ☐, 44, 42

6 Which pattern goes backwards by 3 each time?

A 30, 33, 36, 39
B 15, 13, 11, 9
C 12, 9, 6, 3
D 3, 6, 9, 12

7

69 + ☐ = 80

79 + ☐ = 90

8

22 + 15 = 20 + ☐

66 + 46 =100 + ☐

9

115 + 5 = 100 + ☐

110 + 15 = 100 + ☐

10 Complete the table.

−	100	200	300	400
25				

11 Write a number sentence to match the number line.

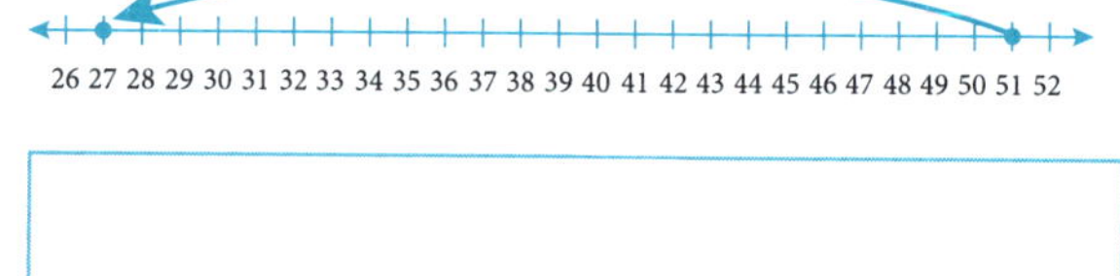

12 There were 18 chairs for 24 children. How many children had to sit on the floor?

13 Complete the table.

×	1	2	3	4
10				

14 The florist needs 10 bunches of roses for Mother's Day. Each bunch has 10 roses. Write a number sentence to show how many roses the florist needs altogether.

NUMBER AND ALGEBRA

1 How many groups of 100 are there in 1000?

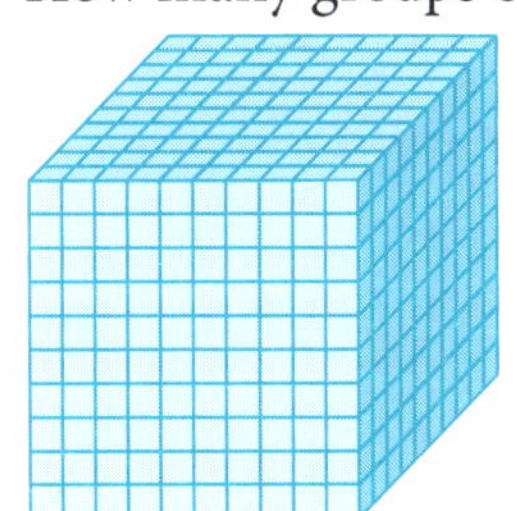

2 Rachel picked 40 lemons off her tree. She will give them to her two neighbours. How many lemons will each neighbour get?

3 Colour one-quarter of the chocolate.

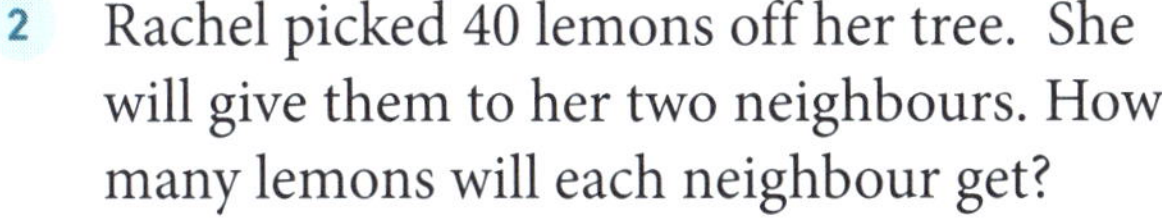

4 John has $2.80. He wants to buy gifts for his two grandmothers. They need to get the same gift. Which gift can he afford?

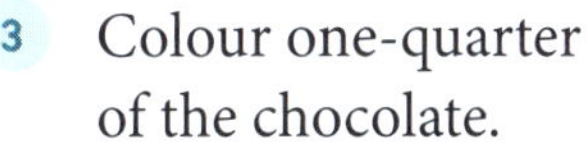

5 Melea has

She needs to buy

How much money will she have left?

MEASUREMENT AND SPACE

6 It is quarter to six. Dinner will be ready in an hour. Draw the hands on the clock to show the time dinner will be ready.

7 School finishes at 3.15. That's an hour from now. What time is it now? Draw the time on the clock.

8 12 September is a Wednesday. What date is the following Saturday?

9 Which shape has an area of 5 square units?

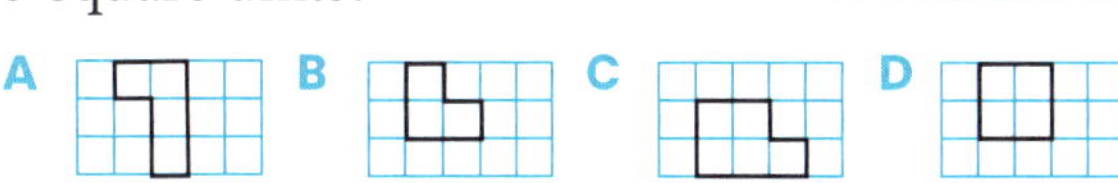

10 Draw the other half of the shape so that both halves are symmetrical.

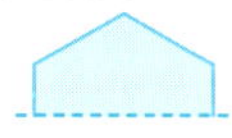

11 Describe this:

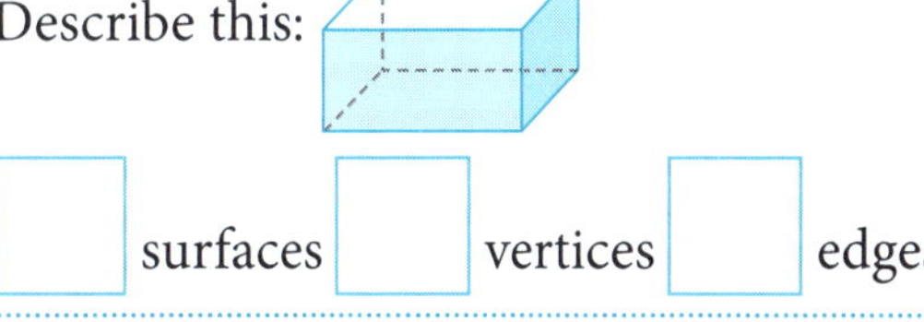

☐ surfaces ☐ vertices ☐ edges

12 In which cell is the black fish?

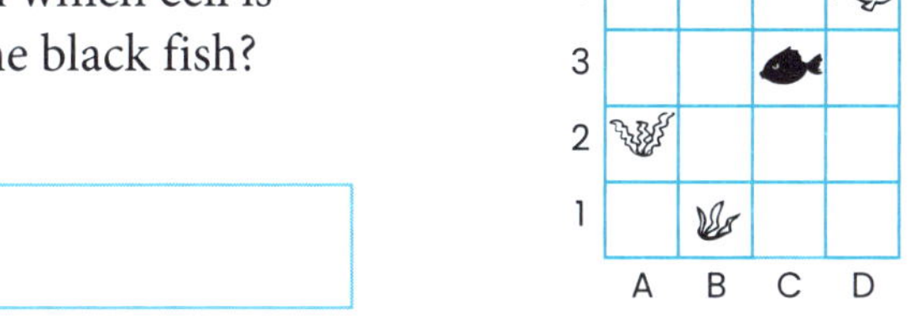

13 Piper folded a rectangle in half and cut out some shapes. Here is her folded rectangle. What does it look like unfolded?

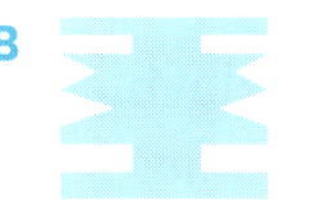

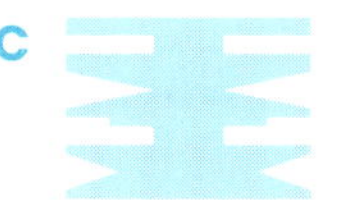

STATISTICS AND PROBABILITY

14 What are the chances that you will throw a six?

A impossible
B one chance in three
C likely
D one chance in six

NUMBER AND ALGEBRA

1 Which of these is 940?

A 900 + 40 B 900 + 10 + 4
C 90 + 40 + 2 D 90 + 40

2 Write the numbers in sequence from smallest to largest.

271, 377, 711, 117

3 What number is exactly halfway between 475 and 535?

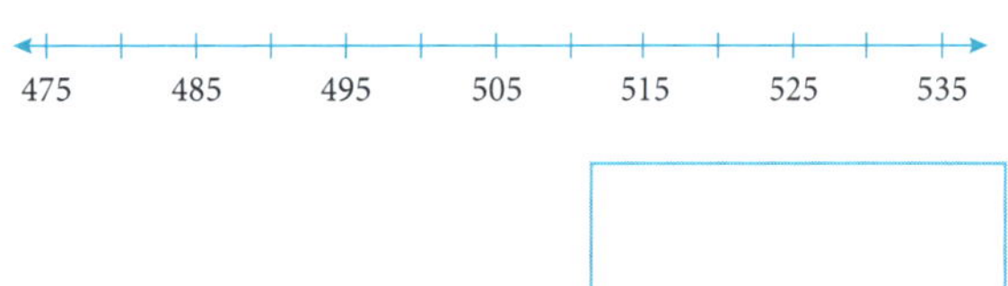

4 What number is exactly halfway between 80 and 160?

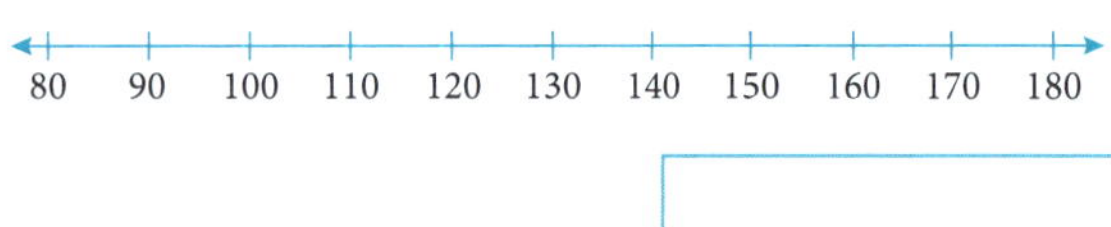

5 Fill in the missing numbers in the pattern.

28, 25, 22, ☐, ☐, ☐, 10, 7

6 Which pattern doubles and adds one each time?

A 2, 4, 6, 8, 10 B 4, 8, 16, 32
C 12, 25, 51, 103 D 2, 6, 14, 30

7

☐ + 55 = 60

☐ + 55 = 70

8

44 + 16 = 40 + ☐

45 + 15 = 40 + ☐

9

120 + 12 = 130 + ☐

119 + 11 = 120 + ☐

10 Complete the table.

−	100	200	300	400
75				

11 There were 25 carrots. The kangaroos ate 20. How many were left?

12 Thirty students from 2W and 2H were on the bus. If ten were from 2W, how many were from 2H?

13 Complete the table.

×	5	6	7	8
10				

14 The box holds 10 cookies. Write a number sentence to show how many cookies are in 4 boxes.

NUMBER AND ALGEBRA

1 Divide 200 into groups of 50. How many groups will you get?

2 Mum has a bag of 24 lollies to share evenly between 5 children.

How many lollies will they each get?

How many lollies will be left over?

3 Heidi made a cake. She gave half to her neighbour. She cut the other half into four equal slices. She ate a slice.
What fraction of the cake is left?

A $\frac{3}{4}$ B $\frac{1}{2}$ C $\frac{3}{8}$ D $\frac{1}{8}$

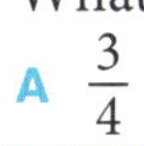
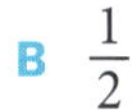

4 Yan has $20.00. She wants to buy two different gifts. Which two gifts can she afford?

5 Zoe needs to buy

$4.40

She has

How much money will she have left?

MEASUREMENT AND SPACE

6 Layla needs to be home in half an hour. What time will that be? Write your answer in words.

7 Mum watches the news at 7 o'clock. That is in fifteen minutes. What time is it now? Write the time in words.

8 12 September is a Wednesday. What date is the previous Saturday?

9 Alex needs to buy ice cream for a party. Which tub should he buy?

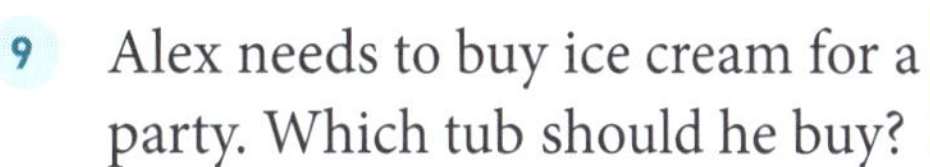

A 

B 

C 

D 

10 Which two shapes join to make this one?

A  B  C D 

11  This object is

A a pentagon. B an octagon.
C a triangle. D a hexagon.

12 Draw the last card.

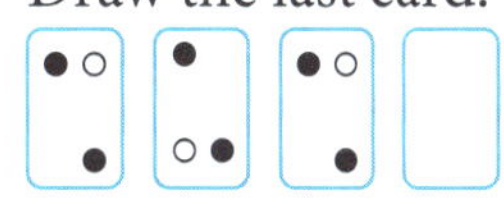

13 A rectangle has been folded in half and some shapes have been cut out. When the paper is unfolded which one will match?

A   B  C 

STATISTICS AND PROBABILITY

14 What are the chances that you will throw a 5?

A one chance in five
B one chance in six

C one chance in three
D very good

Gumleaf Wildlife Park

Show your working out in number sentences or drawings.

NUMBER AND ALGEBRA

1 The park ranger said there were ten cockatoos hiding in two trees. How many cockatoos could there be in each tree? Write all the possible answers.

2 In January the park was caring for fifteen possums injured in a bushfire. Six have been taken back to the bush. How many possums are left?

3 Each of the park's ten kangaroos gets two carrots a week. How many carrots does the park need every week for the kangaroos?

4 The nine black flying foxes eat nectar and pollen from native trees but as a treat the park kitchen staff bought 18 mangoes. How many mangoes will each flying fox get?

5 It costs $10 a day to feed the birds in the aviary. How much does it cost for a week?

MEASUREMENT AND SPACE

6 The park opens at 10:00 and closes at 5:00. How many hours is it open in a day?

7 The aviary is a square pyramid. It is 70 metres tall to the top in the middle and 50 metres long. Draw it on spare paper. Add labels for the measurements.

8 The kangaroo enclosure is the furthest enclosure from the park's entry. Visitors have to walk one kilometre in a direct line to see the kangaroos. On the way they first pass the wombat enclosure on the right then the aviary on the left. Draw and label a picture to show these locations. Use spare paper.

STATISTICS AND PROBABILITY

9 The weather report says there's a good chance it will rain on Sunday. Jade's family does not want to visit the park when it's raining. Should they go on Sunday?

STATISTICS AND PROBABILITY

The graph shows how many people visited the park over a week.
Answer the questions below.

10

a How many people visited on Thursday? ______

b Why do you think Monday is not listed on the graph? ______

c Which day was the busiest at the park? ______

d Which day had the fewest visitors? ______

11 The park ranger asked one hundred park visitors to vote for their favourite mammal at the park. Forty people chose the koalas. Twenty people chose the Tasmanian devils. Five people chose the echidnas. Five people chose the flying foxes. Thirty people chose the wombats.

Draw a graph with labels to show the results of the voting.

12 Write a simple sentence to describe the data on display.

______

NUMBER AND ALGEBRA

1 Which of these is 1914?

A 1000 + 90 + 10 + 4
B 1000 + 900 + 10 + 4
C 1 + 9 + 1 + 4
D 1000 + 900 + 4

2 Write the numbers in sequence from smallest to largest.

88, 67, 98, 77

3 Write the largest number you can make from the digits 1, 9 and 6.

4 What number is exactly halfway between 160 and 240?

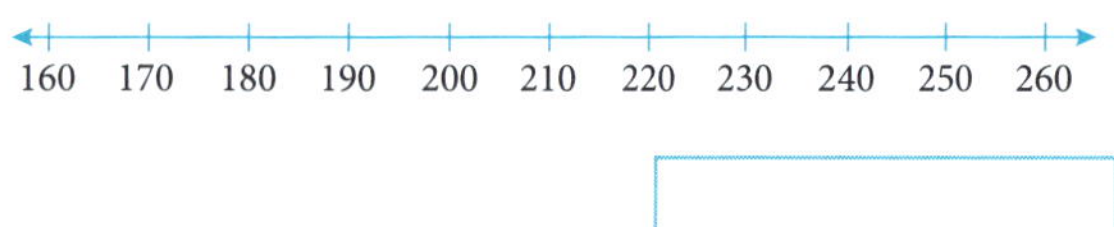

5 Fill in the missing numbers in the sequence.

31, 27, 23, ☐, ☐, 11, 7

6 Which pattern adds 6 each time?

A 6, 13, 20, 27
B 26, 31, 36, 41
C 100, 94, 88, 82
D 66, 72, 78, 84

7

 + 42 = 50

☐ + 52 = 70

8

53 + 17 = 50 + ☐

65 + 25 = 70 + ☐

9

90 + 15 = 100 + ☐

86 + 20 = 100 + ☐

10 Complete the table.

–	500	600	700	800
75				

11 Jeff used 12 litres of paint to paint the house. He had bought 20 litres. How many litres were left over?

12 162 students were in the hall then 31 children went out. Which one helps work out how many children were left in the hall?

A 162 + 31
B 162 + 31 × 2
C 162 ÷ 31
D 162 – 31

13 Complete the table.

×	1	2	3	4
5				

14 One cookie box holds 25 cookies. Write a number sentence to show how many cookies are in 5 boxes.

NUMBER AND ALGEBRA

1 Divide 500 into groups of 100. How many groups are there?

2 Four children need to share six oranges. If each orange is cut in half, how many halves will each child get?

3 What fraction is shaded?

4 Sia has $10.00. She buys

How much change did she get?

5

The money is shared evenly between three children. How much will they each get?

MEASUREMENT AND SPACE

6 David needs to be home in half an hour. What time will that be? Write your answer in words.

7 Dad leaves for work at 6:30. That is in fifteen minutes. What time is it now? Write the time in words.

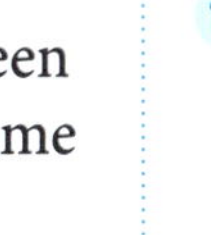

8 15 December is a Tuesday. What date is the following Friday?

9 A marble weighs 20 grams. How many marbles are needed to balance the scale?

10 Which triangles are the same as this one?

A  B  C  D

11 This object 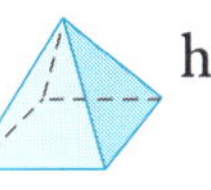 has

☐ surfaces ☐ vertices ☐ edges

12 Draw the last card.

 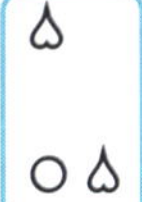  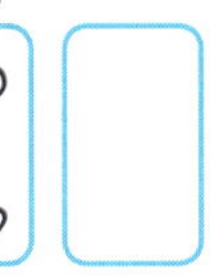

13 A rectangle has been folded in half and some shapes have been cut out. When the paper is unfolded which one will match?

A B  C 

STATISTICS AND PROBABILITY

14 What are the chances that you will throw a 7?

A one chance in five

B one chance in seven

C impossible

D certain

NAPLAN-STYLE TEST 2

1 Some students voted for their favourite colour.

Favourite colour	
yellow	𝍸|||
red	𝍸
blue	𝍸|
green	𝍸|

Which statement is true?

A Twenty-six people voted.
B Blue is more popular than green.
C Yellow is the most popular colour.
D Red is the favourite colour.

2 A litre of milk will weigh

A 100 grams. **B** 1000 kilograms. **C** 10 kilograms. **D** 1000 grams.

3 Freddy bought three loaves of bread.
Two loaves had 23 slices and one loaf had 22 slices.
Which number sentences help Freddy work out how many slices he bought in total?

A $3 \times 23 + 1$ **B** $23 + 23 + 22$ **C** $46 - 22$ **D** $2 \times 23 + 22$

4 Which jigsaw puzzle piece fits into the puzzle?

A

B

C

D

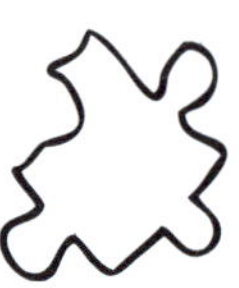

5 Elsa needs to spin an 8 to win a prize at work.

How likely is it that she will spin an 8?

A certain
B impossible
C likely
D unlikely

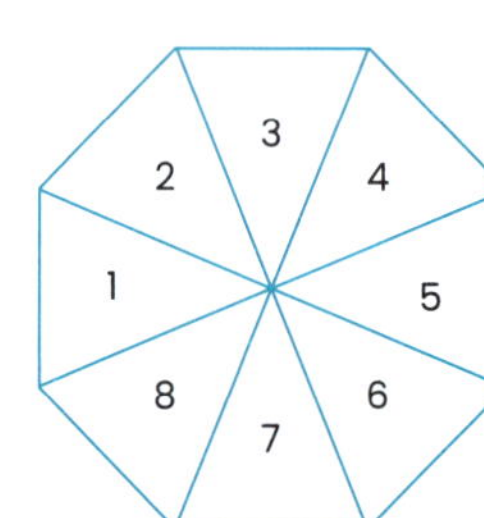

6 How many edges does the pyramid have?

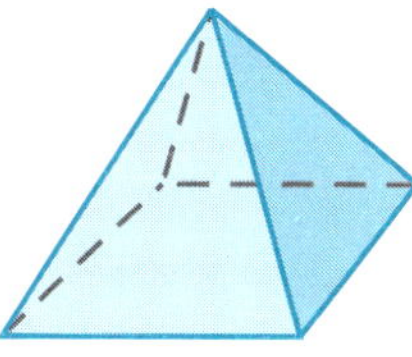

A 4
B 8
C 12
D 5

7 There were 100 people in the art gallery until 15 people left. Which number sentence will help work out how many people were still in the gallery?

A 100 + 15
B 100 × 15
C 100 − 15
D 85 + 15

8 Philippa had 30 marbles. She lost 11 but bought 8 more. How many does she have now?

A 28
B 27
C 26
D 32

9 Yasi, Ahmed, Karim and Habib are brothers. The table shows the years they were born.

Yasi	Ahmed	Karim	Habib
2017	2014	2009	2012

Which brother is the second youngest?

A Yasi B Ahmed C Karim D Habib

10 The class planted 25 wattle trees and 25 banksias. Which one helps you work out how many trees were planted altogether?

A 25 + 25 B 2 + 5 + 25 C 50 − 25 D 25 × 4

11 Kelly earns $10 for every car she washes. How much money did she earn in week 3?

A $40
B $50
C $30
D $20

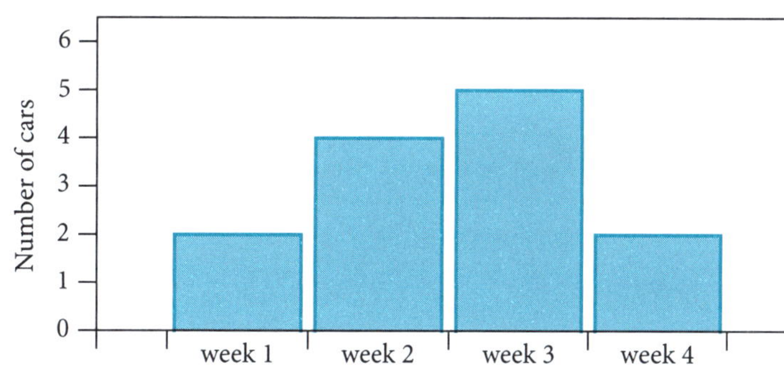

12 The school playground is a rectangle. It has a perimeter of 100 metres.

The shorter sides are each 20 metres long.

What is the length of each longer side?

A 15 m
B 20 m
C 30 m
D 40 m

13 The fraction coloured is

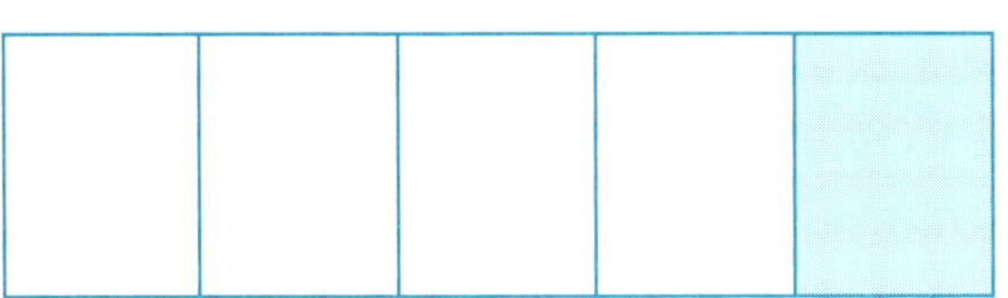

A $\frac{1}{5}$

B $\frac{1}{2}$

C $\frac{1}{4}$

D $\frac{1}{3}$

14 Mum bought 120 bricks to build a path. She only used 98.

Which one helps you work out how many bricks were left over?

A 120 − 98
B 120 + 98
C 120 ÷ 98
D 120 × 98

15 The teacher had twenty sheets of cardboard for five groups of students.

How many sheets did each group get?

A 5 + 5 + 5 + 50
B 20 ÷ 5
C 5 + 20
D 4 ÷ 20

16 What shape is at D2?

A heart
B star
C cross
D triangle

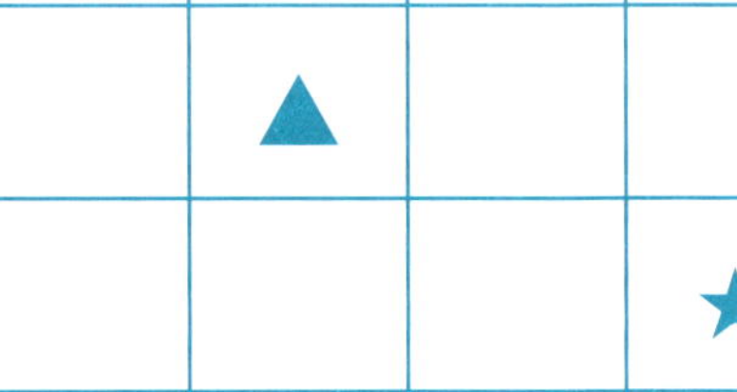

4				✖
3		▲		
2				★
1		♥		
	A	B	C	D

17 These five students are holding hands.

Which child is holding Pow's left hand?

A Mel **B** Brooke

C Anthony **D** Eden

18 What time is shown on the clock?

A quarter to six **B** quarter past six

C quarter to seven **D** quarter past seven

19

The pattern is made by turning a card.

Which card is missing?

A 

B 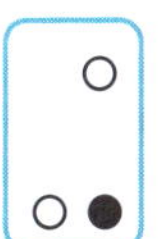

C 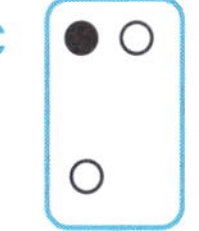

D 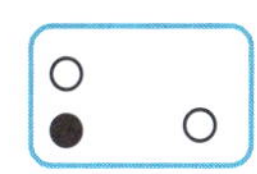

20 Harlow has these coins.

She buys two bananas at 90c each and six apples at 50c each.

How much money does she have left?

A 10c **B** 30c **C** 20c **D** 35c

ANSWERS

Please note: When students are asked to circle or colour a group or shape, or draw something, a sample answer is given but there may be more than one way to correctly answer these questions.

Unit 1A PAGE 10

1. 2, 3; 3, 1
2. B
3. C
4. 53
5. 5
6. D
7. 7
8. 23, 24, 25, 26
9. A
10. 5, 10, 15, 20
11. C

12. 10
13.

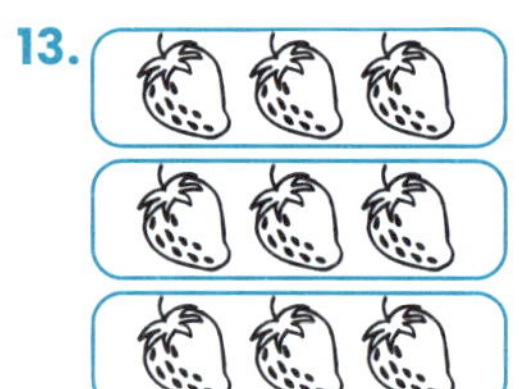

14. D

Unit 1B PAGE 11

1. 6
2. 5
3. B, C
4.

5.

6. two
7.

8. July
9.

10.

11.

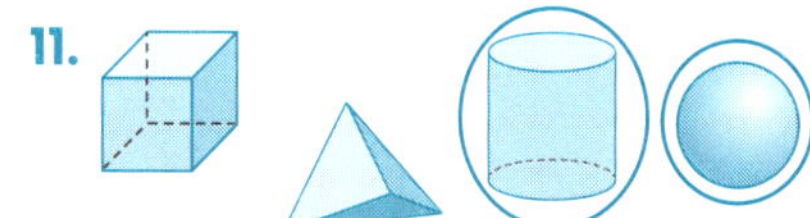

12.

4				
3				
2		★		
1				
	A	B	C	D

13. D
14. A

Unit 1C PAGE 12

1. 12 (12 – 1 + 1 = 12)
2. 22 (12 + 10 = 22)
3. 17 (10 + 7 = 17)
4. 12 divided between 4 children means they get 3 squares each.
5. A
6.

7. C
8. C
9. C

Unit 1D PAGE 13

10. a Parent/teacher to check
    b seven o'clock, nine o'clock, half past four
11. Parent/teacher to check
12. Parent/teacher to check

Unit 2A PAGE 14

1. 1, 8; 2, 6
2. C
3. 423
4. 56 (41 + 15)
5. 5
6. C
7. 5
8. 24, 25, 26, 27
9. C
10. 10, 20, 30, 40
11. D

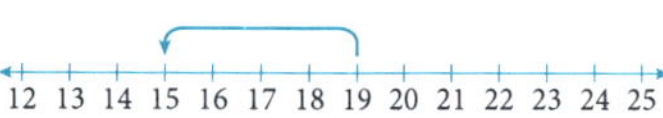

12. 20
13.

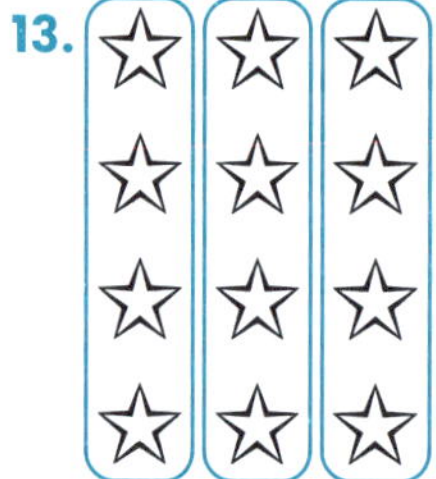

14. B

Unit 2B PAGE 15

1. 4
2. 2
3. B
4. A
5.

6. 8 o'clock
7.

8. November
9. C
10.

11. A

12. 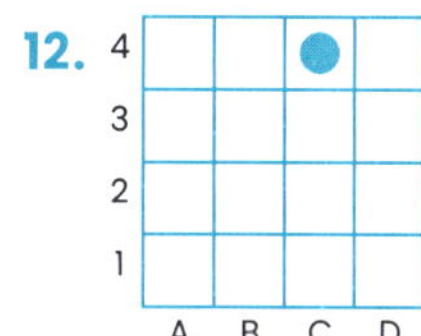

13. C

14. C

Unit 3A PAGE 16

1. 4, 2; 3, 4
2. C
3. 216
4. 37 (19 + 18)
5. 10
6. C
7. 9
8. 26, 27, 28, 29
9. A
10. 18, 28, 38, 48
11. D

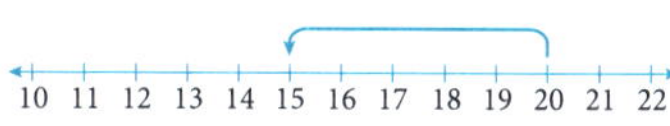

12. 10
13. Parent/teacher to check
14. D

Unit 3B PAGE 17

1. 5
2. B
3. A
4. D
5. Parent/teacher to check
6. twelve o'clock
7. 
8. 30
9. B
10. 

11.

12.

13.

14. 

Unit 3C PAGE 18

1. 12 (1 + 5 + 1 + 5 = 12)
2. 13 (15 – 2 = 13)
3. \$40.00 (\$10 × 4 = \$40)
4. 24 slices (3 × 8 = 24)
5. C
6. 5 kilograms (20 ÷ 4 = 5)
7. 1000 metres or one kilometre (300 + 200 + 300 + 200 = 1000)
8. 4 o'clock
9. A

Unit 3D PAGE 19

10. a Thursday
    b 24 March
    c 27 March
    d Parent/teacher to check
    e 9 times
    f Parent/teacher to check
    g Parent/teacher to check
11. Wednesday
12. Wednesday

Unit 4A PAGE 20

1. 6, 7; 1, 4
2. D
3. 605
4. 58 (40 + 18)
5. 3
6. C
7. C
8. 20, 30, 40, 50
9. B
10. 23, 33, 43, 53
11. D

12. 50
13. Parent/teacher to check
14. B

Unit 4B PAGE 21

1. 

   4
2. 4
3.
4. A
5. Parent/teacher to check
6. half past one or one-thirty
7.
8. December
9. C
10. 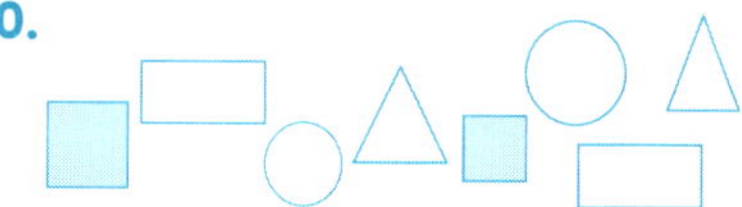
11. 
12. 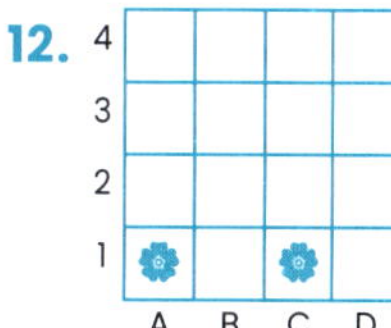
13. 

14.

8

Unit 5A PAGE 22

1. 9, 2; 8, 7
2. C
3. 415
4. 70 (61 + 9)
5. 2
6. C
7. 12
8. 20, 30, 40, 50
9. A
10. 6, 16, 26, 36
11. D

12. 70
13. 10
14. C

Unit 5B PAGE 23

1. 6
2. 12
3. B
4. C
5.    
6. half past two or two-thirty
7.
8. 31
9. C
10. 

11.

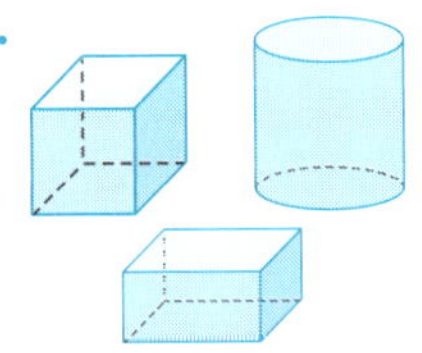

12.

13. 

14. snakes

Unit 5C PAGE 24

1. 4 (4 × 4 = 16)
2. 9 (30 – 21 = 9)
3. 5, 4
4. C
5. 3 each and 2 left over (5 × 3 + 2 = 17)
6. one and a half hours or 1 hour 30 minutes
7. 9
8. B (You can also estimate the time it will take to walk 1 kilometre.)
9. yes

Unit 5D PAGE 25

10. Parent/teacher to check
11. **a** Matt's house
    b supermarket
    c school
    d offices
    e park
    f vet
    g childcare centre
12. Parent/teacher to check

Unit 6A PAGE 26

1. 2, 2; 5, 7
2. D
3. 910
4. 72 (50 + 22)
5. 2
6. ◆ ● ■
7. 22
8. 40, 50, 60, 70
9. 3
10. 4, 14, 24, 34
11. C

12. 50
13. Parent/teacher to check
14. B

Unit 6B PAGE 27

1. 7
2. C
3. 
4. C
5. 

6. half past four or four-thirty
7.
8. February
9. 3
10. A
11. C
12.
13.
14. koala

Unit 7A PAGE 28

1. 132
2. 18, 28, 81
3. C
4. 400
5. 20, 25, 30
6.   
7. 18
8. 200, 300, 400, 500
9. B
10. 2, 2
11. 20 – 3 = 17

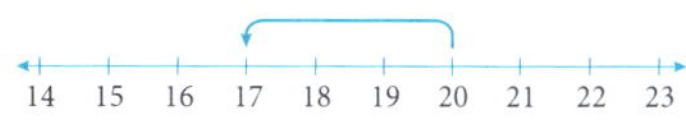

12. B
13. 9
14. B

Unit 7B PAGE 29

1. 

9
2. A
3. D
4. $2.60
5.   
6. half past ten or ten-thirty
7.
8. 14 (5 + 2 + 5 + 2)
9. Tuesday
10. B
11. 8
12. 
13.

14. 4

Unit 7C PAGE 30

1. 20 (15 + 5 = 20)
2. 200 (500 – 300 = 200)
4. 500 (1000 ÷ 2 = 500)
4. C
5. 3 × 4 + 2 = 14
6. 45 minutes (60 – 15 = 45)
7. 5:15 or quarter past five
8. 5:15 or quarter past five
9. D

Unit 7D PAGE 31

10. C
11. A
12 a Parent/teacher to check

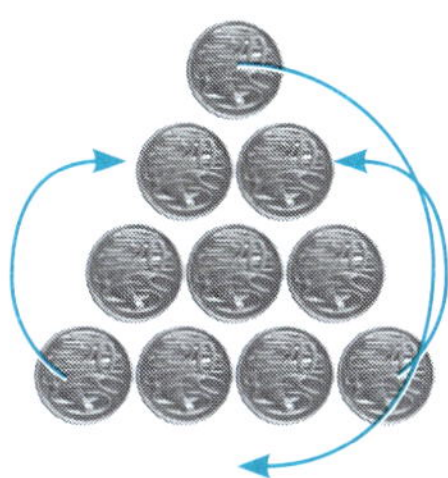

b Parent/teacher to check

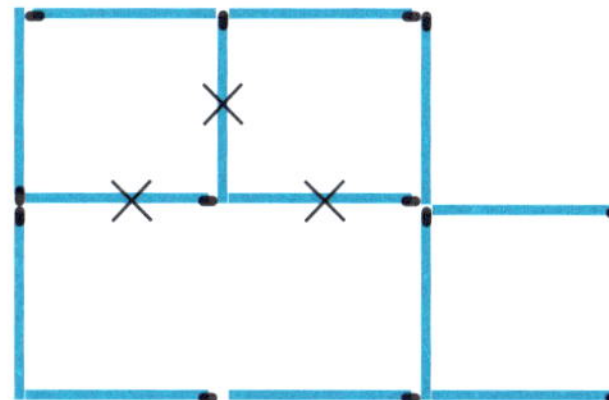

c C

Unit 8A PAGE 32

1. 146
2. 33, 38, 83
3. C
4. 600
5. 3
6. ⊙
7. 14
8. 300, 400, 500, 600
9. C
10. 60, 5
11. 46 – 7 = 39

12. 17
13. 12
14. B

Unit 8B PAGE 33

1. 7 cakes per plate
2. 8
3. A, B, C, D
4. $2, $1.75
5. 50c, 5c

6. 60
7.
8. 12
9. 14 (3 + 4 + 3 + 4)
10. 
11. 16
12. 
13.
14. 3

Unit 9A PAGE 34

1. 211
2. 17, 71, 77
3. C
4. 500
5. 2
6. ●

7. 16
8. 400, 500, 600, 700
9. 3
10. 10, 10
11. 46 – 8 = 38

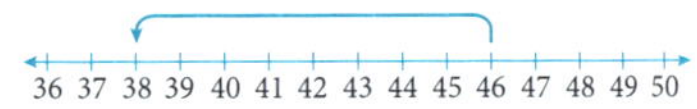

12. 19
13. 15
14. B

Unit 9B — PAGE 35

1.

5

2. 4
3. C
4. $3.30
5.   
6. half past nine or nine-thirty
7.
8. 24
9. 12 squares
10. A, C, E
11. B
12. 
13.
14. B

Unit 9C — PAGE 36

1. elephant's brain
2. 6
3. C
4. D
5. A
6. rhinoceros beetle
7. A
8. 
9. C

Unit 9D — PAGE 37

10. Parent/teacher to check
11. Parent/teacher to check
12. 5B

Unit 10A — PAGE 38

1. 211
2. 33, 34, 43
3. C
4. 300
5. 20, 22, 24
6. ●◆◆
7. 20
8. 450, 550, 650, 750
9. 11
10. 70
11. 72 – 9 = 63

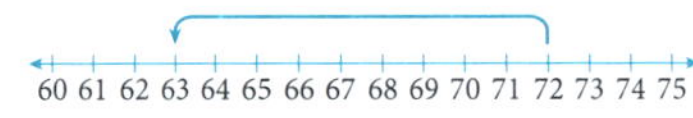

12. 27
13. 18
14. B

Unit 10B — PAGE 39

1.

9

2. 3
3. A
4. $2.50 and $2 or $2.20 and $2.30
5.     
6. half past five or five-thirty
7. 
8. Monday
9. Parent/teacher to check
10. four straight sides of equal length, all angles are equal
11. A
12. 
13.
14. C

Unit 11A — PAGE 40

1. 310
2. 15, 51, 55
3. D
4. seven hundred and fifty-one
5. 38, 45, 52
6. Π
7. 5
8. 150, 250, 350, 450
9. 9
10. 60, 70
11. 38

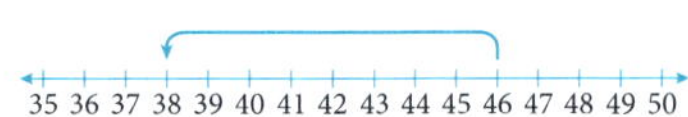

12. 20
13. 16
14. D

Unit 11B — PAGE 41

1. 4

2. 2
3. A, D
4. $3.50 and 50c or $2.50 and $1.50
5. 10c
6. half past eight or eight-thirty
7. half past two or two-thirty
8. 31 October
9. Parent/teacher to check

10. 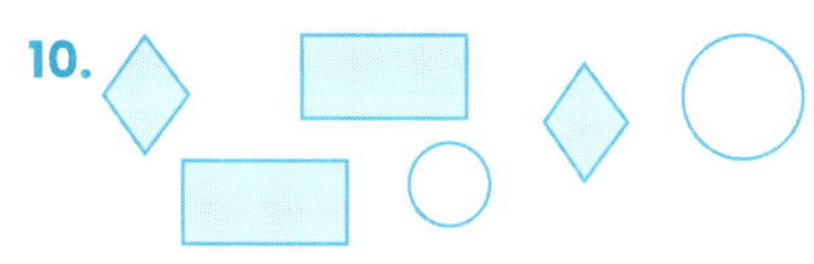

11. D

12. 

13. L Γ

14. D

Unit 11C PAGE 42

1. 17 (4 + 2 + 3 + 2 × 4 = 17)
2. 8 (5 + 3 = 8)
3. 23 (25 – 2 = 23)
4. 60 (100 – 40 = 60)
5. 4 kilometres (8 ÷ 2 = 4)
6. 5 o'clock or 5:00 (7 – 2 = 5)
7. 6 kilometres (3 × 2 = 6)
8. D
9. D

Unit 11D PAGE 43

10. 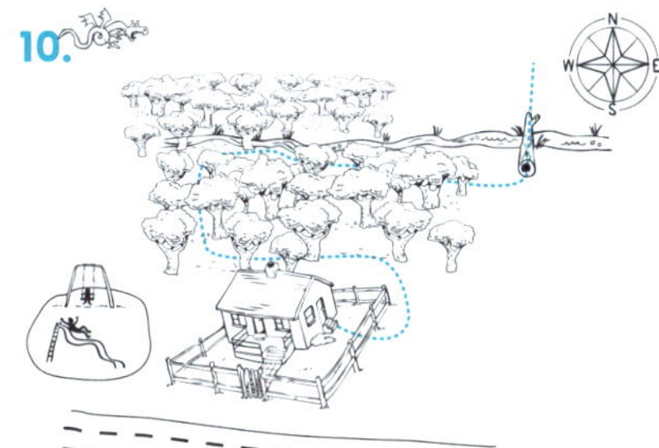

a A
b A
c D
d B
e B

12. Parent/teacher to check

Unit 12A PAGE 44

1. 0, 6, 5; 1, 4, 2
2. 16, 56, 65
3. D
4. nine hundred and twenty-four
5. 53, 50, 47
6. ΘΔ
7. 8
8. 200, 300, 400, 500
9. 100
10. 71, 81
11. 71 – 9 = 62

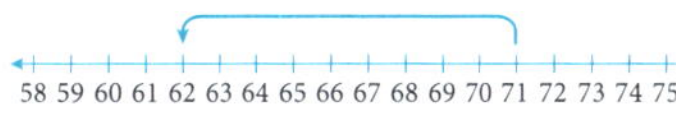

12. 5
13. 24
14. D

Unit 12B PAGE 45

1. 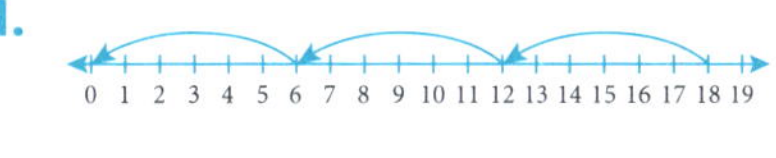

3

2. 7

3. 

4. $6.50
5. 15c
6. half past eleven or eleven-thirty
7. 
8. 1 August
9. 14 (1 + 6 + 1 + 6)
10. This is a square. Its sides are straight and equal in length. All four angles are equal.
11. D
12. 
13. 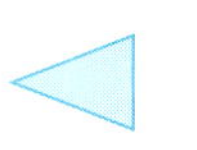 
14. A

Unit 13A PAGE 46

1. A
2. 18, 28, 81, 82
3. B
4. five hundred and forty-three
5. 23, 47
6. 
7. 10
8. 300, 400, 500, 600
9. 20
10. 20, 10
11. 44

12. 5
13. 24
14. C

Unit 13B PAGE 47

1. 3 (18 ÷ 6 = 3)

0 1 2 3 4 5 6 7 8 9 10 11 12 13 14 15 16 17 18 19

2. 11
3. 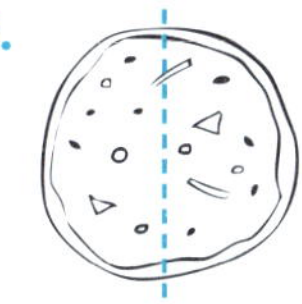 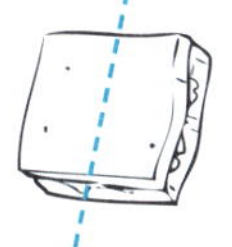

4. $8.15
5. 45c
6. half past seven or seven-thirty
7. 
8. 28 July
9. 6 squares

10. 

11. A

12.

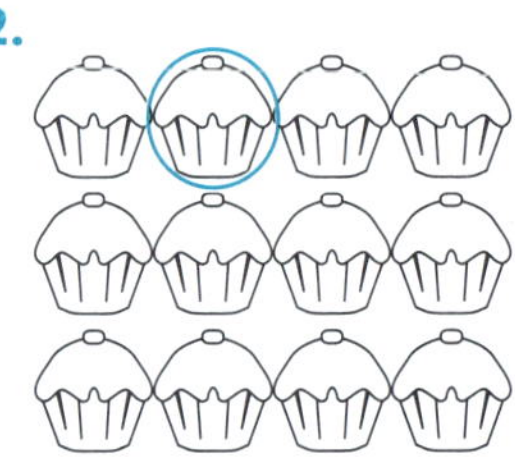

13.

14. B

Unit 13C PAGE 48

1. A
2. B and D
3. C
4. C
5. D
6. C (10 o'clock plus 1 hour 15 minutes = 11:15)
7. autumn
8. September, October, November
9. summer

Unit 13D PAGE 49

10. a 14
    b 24 (14 sunny extra hot and 10 sunny)
    c 5
    d 24 – 5 = 19
    e hot and sunny
    f 29
    g 28
    h It's a leap year.
    i summer
11. Parent/teacher to check
12. Parent/teacher to check

Unit 14A PAGE 50

1. 450
2. D
3. A
4. two hundred and thirty
5. 21, 26, 31
6. 2
7. 6
8. 825, 850, 875, 900
9. 5
10. 5, 5
11. 44

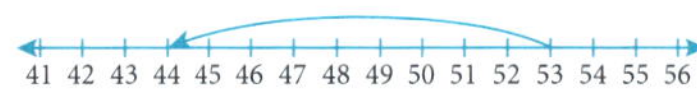

12. 84
13. Parent/teacher to check
14. 24

Unit 14B PAGE 51

1. 10
2. 6
3. Parent/teacher to check
4. $1.55
5.  
6. quarter past four or four-fifteen
7.  
8. June
9. 10 squares
10. They both have four straight sides and four equal angles.
11. A
12. 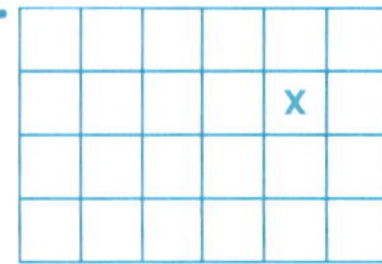
13. B
14. C

Unit 15A PAGE 52

1. nine hundred and four
2. D
3. B
4. two hundred and nine
5. 25, 31
6. 2
7. 8, 18
8. 910, 920, 930, 940
9. 20
10. 5, 5
11. 76

12. 70c
13.  
14. 36

Unit 15B PAGE 53

1. 5
2. a 6 pencils each
   b 2 left over
3. Parent/teacher to check
4. $1.80
5. 

   Parent/teacher to check other alternatives.
6. quarter past nine or nine-fifteen
7. 
8. summer
9. 15 squares
10. They both have four straight sides and four equal angles.

11. 6

12. 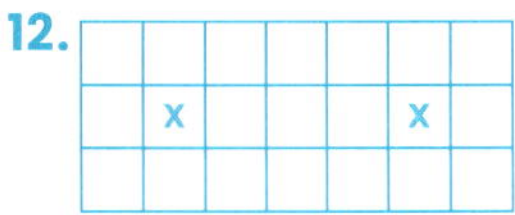

13. C

14. A

Unit 15C PAGE 54

1. D
2. D
3. C
4. B, C
5. a 3
   b 2
6. 37 seconds
7. B
8. A, B, C, F, G, H, I, J, K, L
9. A

Unit 15D PAGE 55

10. a yes
    b no
    c yes
    d yes
    e no
    f yes
11. Parent/teacher to check
12. Parent/teacher to check

NAPLAN-style Test 1 PAGES 56–59

1. C
2. D
3. D
4. B
5. C
6. C
7. C
8. B
9. A
10. A, B, C D
11. D
12. A
13. D
14. B
15. D
16. A
17. D
18. B
19. D
20. B

Unit 16A PAGE 60

1. 89
2. B
3. B
4. nine hundred and eighty-one
5. 13, 10, 7
6. 3
7. 29 + 10 = 39
8. 250, 350, 450, 550
9. 10
10. 20, 20
11. 9
12. 10c
13. 20
14. D

Unit 16B PAGE 61

1. 4
2. 2
3. 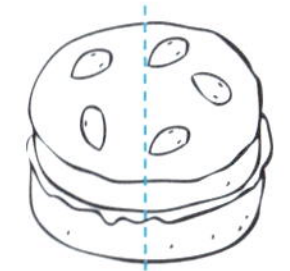
4. $3.60
5. 
6. quarter past one or one-fifteen
7. 
8. 6 kg or 6 kilograms
9. winter
10. 3, 3
11. D
12. A
13. 
14. Tilly 17, Brandon 19, George 25

Unit 17A PAGE 62

1. 329
2. D
3. C
4. four hundred and forty
5. 40, 45, 50
6. 1
7. 42 + 8 = 50
8. 300, 400, 500, 600
9. 1
10. 8, 8
11. 8
12. 25c
13. 5
14. A and D

Unit 17B PAGE 63

1. 8
2. 4
3. 12
4. $2.75
5. 10c (2 × 5c coins or a 10c coin)
6. quarter past twelve or twelve-fifteen
7. 
8. 5 April
9. 16 kg
10. A
11. 8

12. D

13.

14.

Books borrowed in Term 1	Tally	Total
Tilly	卌 ||||	9
Brandon	卌 卌 ||	12
George	卌 卌 ||||	14

Unit 17C PAGE 64

1. 27 (15 + 12 = 27)
2. 9 (25 – 5 – 11 = 9)
3. 1500 or one thousand five hundred (1000 + 500 = 1500)
4. 50 (70 – 20 = 50)
5. half
6. baby carrots
7. 450 litres (470 – 20 = 450)
8. 25 metres (80 – 15 – 15 = 50, 50 ÷ 2 = 25)
9. C

Unit 17D PAGE 65

10. Parent/teacher to check; for example:

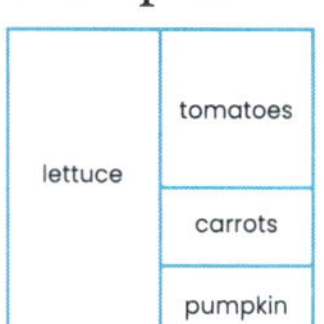

11. **a** half or $\frac{1}{2}$
b one-quarter or $\frac{1}{4}$

12 **a**

b 3

c

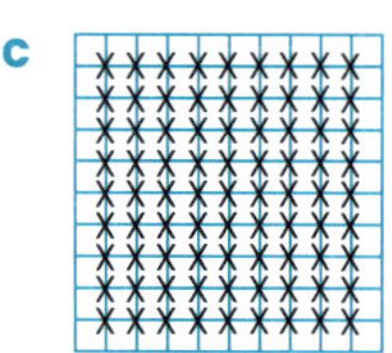

d 81

e 14 November (30 days in September, 31 days in October, 14 days until 14 November)

Unit 18A PAGE 66

1. 607
2. D
3. A
4. eight hundred and ninety-nine
5. 55, 60, 65
6. 3
7. 37 + 9 = 46
8. 400, 500, 600, 700
9. 30
10. 9, 9
11. 6
12. 50c
13. 6
14. A, D

Unit 18B PAGE 67

1. 6
2. 3
3. 6
4. $2.35
5. $2.00
6. quarter past eleven or eleven-fifteen
7. 
8. Saturday
9. A
10. A
11. D
12. A
13.

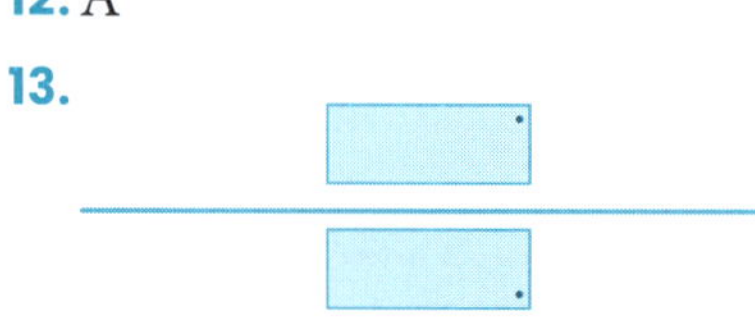

14.

Books borrowed in February	Tally	Total
Jo	卌 卌 |	16
Alice	卌 ||||	9
Misako	||||	4

Unit 19A PAGE 68

1. 543
2. A
3. B
4. 90
5. 55, 65, 75
6. 3
7. 29 + 9 = 38
8. 600, 700, 800, 900
9. 10
10. 7, 7
11. 3
12. $1.50
13. 6
14. 18

Unit 19B PAGE 69

1. 7
2. 10
3. 20
4. $2.80
5. $1.00
6. two
7. 
8. Tuesday
9. B
10. Z
11. D
12.

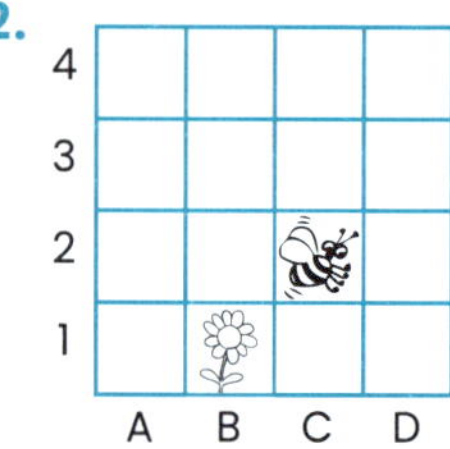

13. 

14. apples

Unit 19C — PAGE 70

1. 30 (24 + 1 + 5 = 30)
2. 25 (55 – 24 – 1 – 5 = 25)
3. 6 (24 ÷ 4 = 6)
4. 12 (24 ÷ 2 = 12)
5. \$48 (24 × 2 = 48)
6. 30 minutes or half an hour
7. 1 litre or 1000 millilitres (4 × 250 = 1000)
8. east
9. D

Unit 19D — PAGE 71

10. Parent/teacher to check
11. a Dinosaur canyon and Australian fossils
    b Dinosaur canyon
    c Dinosaur life cycles
    d Tyrannosaurus rex
12 a Parent/teacher to check
    b Tyrannosaurus rex and Muttaburrasaurus

Unit 20A — PAGE 72

1. 360
2. C
3. A
4. five hundred and seven
5. 75, 85, 95
6. 1
7. 17 + 13 = 30
8. 700, 800, 900, 1000
9. 10, 10
10. 20, 30
11. 23
12. 50c
13. 8
14. \$40.00

Unit 20B — PAGE 73

1. 8
2. 5
3. 6
4. 10
5. 4
6. five or 5
7. 
8. Sunday
9. B
10. C
11. C
12.

4				
3				
2				
1				
	A	B	C	D

13. 
14. hippo

Unit 21A — PAGE 74

1. 65
2. B
3. D
4. 40
5. 50, 60, 70
6. B
7. 19 + 6 + 7 = 32
8. 100, 200, 300, 400
9. 10, 20
10. 44, 33
11. 12
12. 10c
13. 9
14. A

Unit 21B — PAGE 75

1. 9
2. 2 (18 pies divided by 9 children = 2 each)
3. 24
4. \$2.60
5. 2
6. seven or 7
7. 
8. Friday
9. C
10. B
11. C
12. 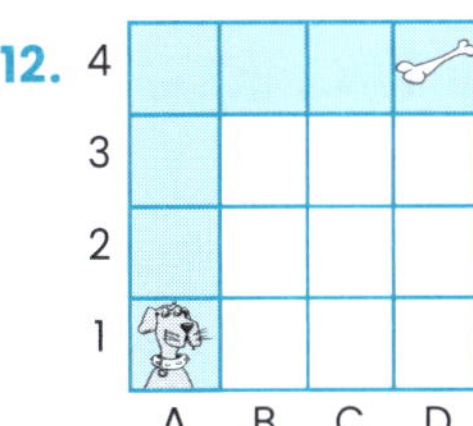

13. 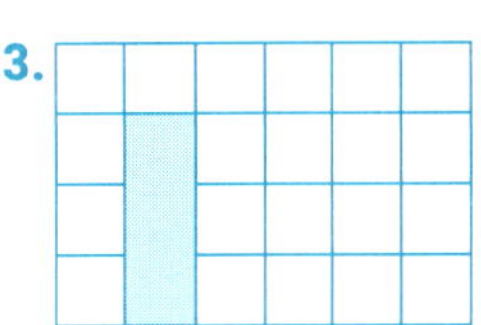
14. tropical

Unit 21C — PAGE 76

1. 2 weeks and 6 days or 20 days (3 + 7 + 7 + 3 = 20)
2. 12 kilometres (2 + 4 + 2 + 4 = 12)
3. 5 years (12 – 7 = 5)
4. 25 (5 × 5 = 25)
5. 3 (20 slices take away Dad's 5 leaves 15 slices and 15 – 12 = 3)
6. C (8 o'clock plus 45 min = 8:15)
7. 3 kilometres (12 ÷ 4 = 3)
8. 500 grams (250 × 2 = 500)
9. B

Unit 21D PAGE 77

10. a C
b C
c B

11. a, b, c, d Parent/teacher to check
e A
f north

12. Parent/teacher to check. Come in entrance. Go past reception on the right. Turn left and go north towards the Nature Centre. Turn right after the Nature Centre. The playground is at the end of the road.

Unit 22A PAGE 78

1. D
2. D
3. C
4. 0 or zero
5. 1, 3, 5, 7, 9
6. B (Did you work out the rule for D? It's double + 1.)
7. 9 + 5 + 8 = 22
8. 75, 175, 275, 375
9. 11, 1
10. 10, 20
11. 12
12. no
13. 6
14. B

Unit 22B PAGE 79

1. 12
2. 4
3. B
4. 10
5. yes
6. 6:00
7. A
8. Tuesday 31 March
9. B
10. 4, 4
11. D
12. e.g. 14 squares

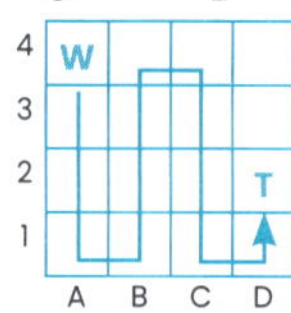

Parent/teacher to check

13.

14.

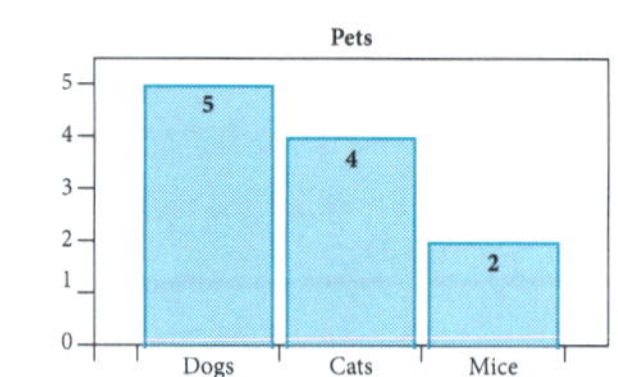

Unit 23A PAGE 80

1. B
2. A
3. D
4. 40
5. 35, 25, 15
6. C
7. 66 + 6 + 4 =76
8. 170, 270, 370, 470
9. 14, 12
10. 20, 30
11. 12
12. 30c
13. 5
14. 88

Unit 23B PAGE 81

1. 14
2. 3
3. B
4. 5
5. no
6. 7:00
7. 12
8. Monday
9. D
10.

11. C
12.

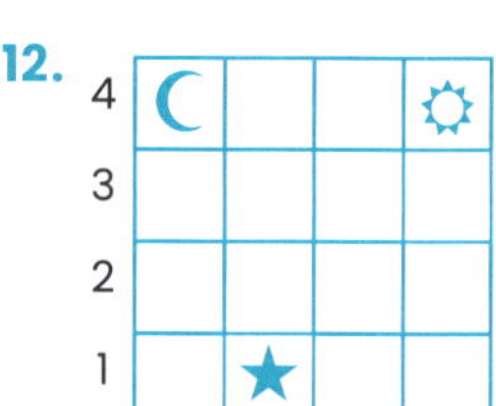

13.

14.

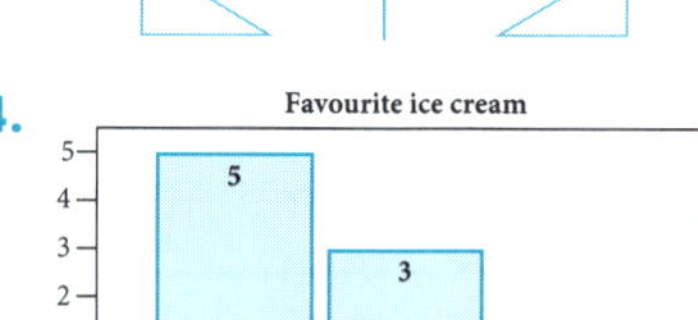

Unit 23C PAGE 82

1. $40.00 ($20.00 + $20.00)
2. $2.00 (20 – 18 = 2)
3. $20.00 (4 × 5 = 20)
4. $5.00 (10 ÷ 2 = 5)
5. $1.50
6. $35.00 (5 × 7 = 35)
7.

8. east
9. C

Unit 23D PAGE 83

10. a 1 × $2 coin
b 40 × 5c coins

11. a 20 × 5c coins
b 10 × 10c coins
c 20 × 10c coins
d 4 × 50c coins

12. 5c echidna; 10c lyrebird; 20c platypus; 50c emu and kangaroo

Unit 24A PAGE 84

1. C
2. A
3. D
4. 70
5. 6, 9, 12
6. D
7. 2, 2
8. 195, 295, 395, 495
9. 4, 6
10. 30, 40
11.

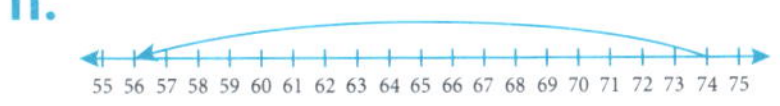

12. yes
13. 8
14. 44

Unit 24B PAGE 85

1. 13
2. 10
3. B
4. $7.80
5. no
6. 03:45
7.

8. D
9. Tuesday 31 May
10. It has 6 straight sides of equal length and 6 corners or angles of equal size.
11.

12. C
13.

14. pears; parent/teacher to check graph

Unit 25A PAGE 86

1. D
2. D
3. B
4. 3 or 3 ones
5. 80, 75, 70
6. D
7. 10, 20
8. 185, 285, 385, 485
9. 11, 6
10. 30, 40
11. 6
12. yes
13. 7
14. $3 \times 22 = 66$

Unit 25B PAGE 87

1. 11
2. 10
3. D
4. $6.50
5. $1.50
6. 4:00
7.
8. Monday
9. C
10. A
11. 9
12.
13. D
14. dolphin; parent/teacher to check graph

Unit 25C PAGE 88

1. 400 grams ($200 \times 2 = 400$)
2. 35 grams ($100 - 65 = 35$)
3. 5
4. 125 grams ($250 \div 2 = 125$)
5. $5.80 ($2.50 + 1.50 + 1.80 = 5.80$)
6. 6:00 or 6 o'clock (15 min + 15 min = 30 min; 5:30 + 30 min = 6:00)
7. 5:00 or 5 o'clock (start cooking 5:15, start preparing 5:00)
8. D
9. A

Unit 25D PAGE 89

10. a chocolate
    b vanilla sponge
    c chocolate
    d $6.00
    e 25 ($1 + 3 + 4 + 11 + 6 = 25$)
11. Parent/teacher to check
12. Parent/teacher to check

Unit 26A PAGE 90

1. B
2. 270

235 245 255 265 270 275 285

3. A
4. 30
5. 14, 21, 28
6. C
7. 20, 20
8. 190, 290, 390, 490
9. 12, 10
10. 50, 60
11. 2
12. 5
13. 7
14. $20 \times 2 = 40$

Unit 26B PAGE 91

1. 15
2. 10
3. C
4. yes

5. $0 or zero or nothing

6. 

7. 12:45 or quarter to one

8. Sunday

9. D

10. circle

11.

12.

13. 

14. bees; parent/teacher to check graph

Unit 27A PAGE 92

1. C
2. 960
3. 12
4. 190

5. 37, 33, 29
6. C
7. 18, 18
8. 200, 300, 400, 500
9. 10, 10
10. 90, 100, 110, 120
11. 86 – 17 = 69
12. 9
13. 9
14. 5 × 3 = 15

Unit 27B PAGE 93

1. 9
2. 12
3. C
4. $6.65
5. 5c

6. 

7. 2:30
8. Thursday
9. 35 degrees, yes
10. 

11. 5 surfaces, 6 vertices, 9 edges

12. 

13. A, D
14. penguins; parent/teacher to check graph

Unit 27C PAGE 94

1. 27 (14 + 13 = 27)
2. 12 (28 – 16 = 12)
3. 20 (4 × 5 = 20)
4. 18 (3 × 6 = 18)
5. $58.90 (22.50 + 36.40 = 58.90)
6. 5 (10 ÷ 2 = 5)
7. 3 kilograms (29 – 26 = 3)
8. four and a half kilometres (2 km + $2\frac{1}{2}$ km = $4\frac{1}{2}$ km)
9. A (or B)

Unit 27D PAGE 95

10. 0, 9, 5, 1, 3, 2, 4
11 a blue
   b red
12 a Parent/teacher to check
   b 9
   c yellow
   d Parent/teacher to check

Unit 28A PAGE 96

1. C
2. C
3. 731
4. 170

5. 50, 48, 46
6. C
7. 11, 11
8. 17, 12
9. 20, 25
10. 75, 175, 275, 375
11. 51 – 24 = 27
12. 6
13. 10, 20, 30, 40
14. 10 × 10 = 100

Unit 28B PAGE 97

1. 10
2. 20
3.
4. 2 roses
5. 60c
6.
7.
8. 15 September
9. C
10.
11. 6 surfaces, 8 vertices, 12 edges
12. C3
13. C
14. D

Unit 29A PAGE 98

1. A
2. 117, 271, 377, 711
3. 505

4. 120

80 90 100 110 **120** 130 140 150 160 170 180

5. 19, 16, 13
6. C
7. 5, 15
8. 20, 20
9. 2, 10
10. 25, 125, 225, 325
11. 5
12. 20
13. 50, 60, 70, 80
14. $4 \times 10 = 40$

Unit 29B PAGE 99

1. 4
2. 4, 4
3. C
4. hand cream and candle
5. 60c
6. quarter past seven or seven-fifteen
7. quarter to seven or six forty-five
8. 8 September
9. B
10. D
11. D
12.
13. C
14. B

Unit 29C PAGE 100

1. 0 + 10, 1 + 9, 2 + 8, 3 + 7, 4 + 6, 5 + 5, 6 + 4, 7 + 3, 8 + 2, 9 + 1, 10 + 0
2. 9 ($15 - 6 = 9$)
3. 20 ($10 \times 2 = 20$)
4. 2 ($18 \div 9 = 2$)
5. \$70 ($7 \times 10 = 70$)
6. 7 hours (10 am to 12 = 2 hours, 12 to 5 pm = 5 hours, Total = 7 hours)
7. 70 m 50 m
8. Parent/teacher to check
9. no

Unit 29D PAGE 101

10. a 20
    b The park is closed on Monday and so it has no visitors.
    c Sunday
    d Wednesday
11. Parent/teacher to check
12. Parent/teacher to check

Unit 30A PAGE 102

1. B
2. 67, 77, 88, 98
3. 961
4. 200

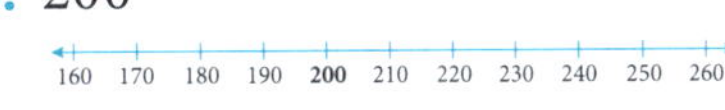

5. 19, 15
6. D
7. 8, 18
8. 20, 20
9. 5, 6
10. 425, 525, 625, 725
11. 8 litres
12. D
13. 5, 10, 15, 20
14. $5 \times 25 = 125$

Unit 30B PAGE 103

1. 5
2. 3
3. half or $\frac{1}{2}$ or $\frac{3}{6}$
4. 5c
5. 70c
6. quarter past ten or ten-fifteen
7. quarter past six or six-fifteen
8. 18 December
9. 5
10. C, D
11. 5, 5, 8
12.

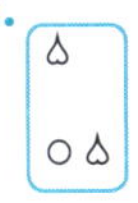

13. B
14. C

NAPLAN-style Test 2 PAGES 104–107

1. C
2. D
3. B, D
4. B
5. D
6. B
7. C
8. B
9. B
10. A
11. B
12. C
13. A
14. A
15. B
16. B
17. C
18. C
19. C
20. D

NOTES

NOTES

NOTES